PARADOXOLOGY

PARADOXOLOGY

Spirituality in a Quantum Universe

Miriam Therese Winter

ORBIS BOOKS

Maryknoll, New York 10545

Library of Congress Cataloging-in-Publication Data

Winter, Miriam Therese.
    Paradoxology / Miriam Therese Winter.
       p. cm.
    Includes bibliographical references.
    ISBN 978-1-57075-817-1 (pbk.)
    1. Religion and science. 2. Quantum theory – Religious aspects – Christianity. I. Title.
    BL240.3.W545 2009
    230 – dc22

                                      2008034411

Contents

Introduction

We followed Alice down the rabbit hole and through the looking glass during our flights of fancy, once upon a time. We even joined Dorothy and Toto for a romp around the Land of Oz and a cross-cultural immersion. But when we returned to reality, we knew the difference between make-believe and what it would take to make sense of the everyday world in which we were living. Not any more.

Today the thin line separating fairy tale from fact in a quantum society is permeable and translucent. The more we hear of the new science, which is not really new, just new to us, the more we feel like we've fallen asleep and been jostled awake in the dreamtime. Like Alice, we are at a loss when faced with "the effect of living backwards" and having to deal with the jabberwocky of an unpredictable, inexplicable quantum universe.

Even with the help of those *Star Trek* episodes that gave us a vocabulary, updated our cosmology, and opened our minds to the possibility of life on other planets, sometimes we too just want to say: "There's no use trying, one can't believe impossible things."[1]

Here then is the first suggestion on how to proceed through this book. Forget about believing. Some things have to be wrestled with in the heart, not in the head. Suspend belief or disbelief long enough to consider the questions and allow yourself a momentary glimpse of the other side of the issues, or the other side of the universe, or the other side of the tracks.

This openness is essential. So much of quantum theory goes against what is self-evident and, consequently, boggles the mind. Once we step through the portal into a quantum universe, we enter into a more whimsical world where the unpredictable is certain, the uncertain is predictable, and the only constant is change.

We live in a quantum world, whether or not we know it. To be unaware does not change the fact that a quantum-based reality is redefining our lives. We can't take anything for granted anymore. The foundations we have come to depend on have already started to crumble, and we will not hold them together by doing what we did in the past.

Our institutions are steeped in paradigm. Quantum reality, however, is filled with paradox. This calls for a radically new approach to seeing and being in the world and understanding our place within it. We have to begin to re-orient ourselves so that who we are and the values we hold retain some form of stability in a world that is in flux.

Paradox, by definition, is chaotic and disorienting. It overturns expectations, has no sense of tradition, and cannot conform to rules. Paradox surrounds us, and yet we continue to move forward in our usual orderly fashion, according to set patterns programmed to take us step by step from one paradigm shift to another. Paradox, on the other hand, proceeds by leaps and bounds. How do we handle this conundrum, which is also a paradox? I have asked myself these questions, and the result has been this book.

This is not a book about science. It is a book about spirituality in a quantum universe. It brings science and spirituality together to explore what they can contribute to making all things new. Here is a second suggestion for the reader. Take the text personally. Wrestle with what may be new ideas and consider living with the questions. That is what I had to do, and because what is presented here has been filtered through my experience, you will have to peel that part away and replace it with experiences and questions of your own.

By situating spirituality within a quantum universe, we are forced to look at the bigger picture and reconsider everything, from the microcosmic subatomic world, which remains invisible, to the macrocosmic universe, which is continually expanding and forever beyond our reach. Where is God in all of this becomes a relevant question. Who is God for me in a world that is different from the one where we first met is a question we will have to address, each in our own way.

What does God require of me in the world that is emerging? What does it mean to be a person of faith, and who is the one to take the measure of our fidelity? In a paradoxical universe, the answers to these perennial questions may not be what we expect.

This book is about discovering, and subsequently deepening, a viable spirituality in our twenty-first-century world. Its aim is to help us realize that we who are people of faith cannot continue to practice our faith in isolation anymore. A quantum universe is telling us that we are all connected, that the God of one is the God of all, that diversity is a blessing, that the suffering of any of Earth's people or any part of the planet is a desecration to us all.

To think and act wholistically means broadening our perspective. One way we might approach this is to immerse ourselves in the quantum energy around us and

within us and to learn to see the Holy Spirit as that primal energy's source. Chaos, consciousness, connection,
as well as coincidence, creation, and celebration are characteristic of a quantum Spirit exuding energy. In quantum
spirituality, they manifest the presence of the Divine in
our midst. Words that are part of quantum mechanics
have been appropriated and reinterpreted as gifts and fruits
of a quantum Spirit permeating quantum lives.

The primary purpose of this book is to jumpstart us
individually in a new direction, to encourage us to look at
life through another pair of lenses that will help us see so
much more than we ever have before.

Along with an effort to put into words a paradigm shift
beyond paradigm comes an invitation to wrestle with paradox as paradigmatic and to realize that paradox is, most
likely, the prevailing paradigm. When paradox sets the pa-
rameters, nothing stays the same, because everything is
in flux.

What are the implications here for that which we say
can never change, and what exactly is that? Whatever
is true of life itself can be said of spirituality, even of
prayer and praise. The ancients have always understood
the organic relationship between paradox and praise.

Spirituality in a quantum universe introduces us to
paradox and re-envisions praise. It says, without equivo-
cation, that life itself is liturgy, simply because liturgy is
life. Life gives living testimony to an incarnate, indwelling
Spirit. All that is, by its very existence, is embodied praise.

Paradox. Doxology. Paradoxology. Life is paradoxical.
Paradox is doxological. At the core of spirituality in a quantum world is paradoxology. It means a universe in the grip
of grace. It is universal praise.

Part One

Quantumstuff

Chapter 1

The Amazing *Para* Maze

Paradoxology. About twenty years ago, this strange, wise, wonderful word appeared in a flash of insight and took up residence in me. I did not know what to do with it, so I let it settle there in the soft underbelly of my spirit. Like a sacred talisman infused with shamanic energy, this shard of the Holy Spirit, cautiously yet consistently, contributed to what I now would call a radical change in perception. It helped me see what I needed to see and encouraged me to embrace it.

It all came together for me one day in a classroom filled with students. While speaking about something I do not recall, I heard myself pose these questions:

Why are the liturgies I celebrate called paraliturgy?

Why are the biblical stories I tell called paraphrase?

There it was, the dilemma, and it is one that affects us all. I had come to the realization that the designation *para* is simply code for exclusion. Categorically, and often irrevocably, it situates the dynamics of praise within a scheme of things that is already well established and constructs the criteria for legitimacy to substantiate its claim. Then I heard Spirit say to me: *"Para* is what you are called to do. Re-imagine *para."* That moment marks a turning point in what I call my "paraphase."

The use of *para* vacillates in intent in our common vocabulary. Note the meaning of paragon, parachute, paramedic, on the one hand, and parasite, paranoid, paranormal, on the other. To be offered a parasol on a hot, sunny day elicits a very different response than to be given the news that a loved one is now a paraplegic. *Para* swings back and forth in delineating one thing from another, as in paradigm and paradox. Language meant to clarify is riddled with an ambivalence that is unpredictable. These are characteristics attributed to a quantum universe and to paradoxology. What is supposed to be paradigmatic is paradoxical.

The use of *para* may indicate something negative or positive, rock solid or elusive, a requirement or an appendage. When added to liturgy, it implies something of lesser value, not canonically valid, not the real thing. How ironic. In ancient times *para* was closely aligned to rites and rituals that celebrated life. An intimate relationship between life and the sacred was perceived by many to be at the very core of reality.

The *rishis*, seers in India to whom the wisdom of the Vedas was revealed thousands of years ago, knew of and experienced an additional state of consciousness that was believed to be sacred. They considered it a unifying force within the universe, and they called it *para*.[2] In Vedic philosophy — *Veda* means wisdom, or science — *Parama* means Supreme and *Paramatma* Supreme Soul. *Paramanus*, invisible entities with no inside or outside and no conceivable mass, constitute the physical realm wherein existence is made visible.[3]

Para is inherently sacred to Christianity as well. Paramount in Christian tradition are the parables of Jesus, those unique morality tales rooted in lived experience that are central to his teaching; and paradise, either the Garden of Eden of "once upon a time" or heaven of "happily ever after," to which we aspire; and Paraclete, God's indwelling Spirit, ever present and divine. Paraclete, paradise, parable are paradoxical to the core and also paradigmatic within our Christian tradition. This rattles the rules of logic, but makes perfect sense in a quantum universe. At the very heart of our Christian faith, paradox is paradigm.

Paradigm and Paradox

Reason and Imagination. Theme and Improvisation. Structure and Chaos. Security and Surprise. It is a challenge to navigate between life-altering alternatives, like rules and regularity on the one hand and freedom of spirit on the other. Sometimes we stay within the lines, at other times, though not often enough, we bravely step outside the box to fly high or free fall or float along unencumbered. We cannot always follow the means and methods we prefer, even with freedom to choose. Fundamental responsibilities or the implications of other choices may have already prescribed our path. We, especially women, usually enter the political arena, the workplace, the ad hoc committee, or the sacramental setting after the agenda is already set and impervious to change.

Those who are marginal, for whatever reason, get stuck at a predetermined point within the dominant paradigm, where far too often they remain and are unable to get anywhere. Welcome to America, where everyone is equal and everyone is free, yet everyone is not. Welcome to the paradox within the paradigm. On the other hand, there are significant underlying changes going on all around us: paradigmatic and paradoxical shifts in human consciousness, in science and spirituality, in our understanding of the universe, in our relationship to planet Earth, and in the socio-political aspirations of a growing number of nation-states all around the globe.

We encounter paradigm daily in the norms and expectations, roles and regulations of religion and society. We speak of "prevailing paradigm" to indicate the status quo, and "paradigm shift" when one controlling standard is replaced by another. Patriarchy remains the dominant paradigm on the macro level, even as lesser paradigm shifts pose challenges from within. Paradigm is clear and convincing and difficult to remove. Paradox, on the other hand, is contradictory and unbelievable, absurd and often compelling, impossible but true. It projects the tension of opposites that are held simultaneously and is therefore given short shrift by the logical Western mind. We come up against it everywhere, and more often than not we dismiss it by saying, that's just the way it is, or, it's a mystery.

Where this is evident today is in the institutional church. The dance between paradox and paradigm goes all the way back to the beginning. The New Testament Book of Acts shows us two different models of the nascent church in Jerusalem. The first is the church in its infancy, shortly after the death and resurrection of Jesus. The second reflects a more institutionally regulated church in the process of coming of age (Acts 2:43–47; 5:1–11).

We can feel the exuberance of a community still caught up in the free-flowing Spirit of Pentecost in the earlier account. Filled with awe at the turn of events following the death of their leader, they continue to feel his presence every time they sit down to a meal, sense his empowering spirit among them, sharing and shaping their lives. They remember and tell stories of how much Jesus meant to them, and their time together culminates in an outpouring of praise. Spontaneously, generously, gladly, they begin to move toward a life in common, keeping only what is necessary and giving the rest to the poor. In the context of this community, the primacy of paradox would have been understood.

The second narrative records an occurrence within the same community, but at a later time. Clearly, a lot has changed. Ananias and his wife, Sapphira, sell a piece of property, but secretly set some money aside before giving the rest to the church. When confronted by Peter, Ananias denies any wrongdoing. The scene reads like a trial before a judge without a jury. When Peter accuses Ananias of sinning against God, Ananias is terrified and drops dead on the spot. Unaware of what has happened, Sapphira appears, is interrogated, and also lies to Peter. The text includes these chilling words from the head of the apostolic church: "Those who buried your husband are coming now for you." She dies of fright and is buried. The final words of this passage read: "And great fear seized the whole church and all who heard of these things." The narrative ends with two dead bodies and everyone terrified. Now to which of these two congregations would you prefer to belong?

We need to ask ourselves questions such as these. What exactly is the lesson here? The behavior of Peter is light-years removed from the community's earlier ethos and from the compassion of Jesus, who took the side of the outcast, who was quick to forgive and would always give the sinner a second chance. Where is the love? The mercy?

Why were husband and wife reluctant to stand up and tell the truth? Had they decided to leave the church? Did they keep the money to support themselves once they were on their own? Was there a structure already in place that made it unsafe to say so? It is time we refuse to accept disempowering models that mimic community, time to reject outrageous behavior from those in leadership roles.

These two early portraits exemplify a contrast in approach to what it means to be church. For much of our lives we move between paradox and paradigm. What holds everything together, the times we tend to do what is right and those times we utterly fail, is unconditional love. Jesus tells us to love in a way that casts out fear, creates community, and helps us make a change in the world by changing our own worldview. Now, more than ever, we need to choose that paradoxological alternative we call life.

Dominant powers are captivated and driven by paradigm. Those with a different vision are drawn to paradox. There is a disconnect today between how life is unfolding, organically and haphazardly, and the way authoritative aspects of religion and society feel it has to be.

We are battered by internal feelings and by external forces, by programs that dissemble and trends that paralyze, but we can also feel the effects of a loving energy disseminated through countless grassroots initiatives of justice and peace. As discordant voices rise from among disenchanted peoples, prevailing paradigms will fall and controlling constructs crumble. Remember, paradoxically, it is from the ashes that life begins anew.

We are in the midst of a clash between commingling worldviews, one with a lengthy history, the other making no sense at all in light of what went before. Life in a quantum universe is pulsating with paradox, making it all the more hospitable to intuitives and mystics, to dreamers and misfits, and to those who are prone to make mistakes but are willing to try again.

A Parallel Universe

It is like a secret garden, this parallel universe, as wide as from here to the Milky Way and as intimate as a prayer. It is where I go when I'm running on empty or find I am filled to the brim with feelings that are driving me up the wall. Ever since I was a very young child, I have slipped in and out of our everyday world, crossing the threshold through those thin places where visible and invisible intersect. I withdraw in order to make meaning of a memory or a moment and return refreshed and enriched. Each of us has our own way of dealing with the world we live in. Sometimes this overlaps with the way we interact with the Divine. My way is multifaceted and firmly anchored at every turn in deep, cosmological roots.

Once upon a time — I can't think of a better way to begin — there was a tiny garden near the corner of a dead-end street that came to a halt in a junkyard, a mill factory, and the stagnant waters of the Dundee Canal, which, when they felt up to it, slid into the Passaic River, a stone's throw from the Big Apple and light years away from its verve. Welcome to my secret garden, the source of my grandmother's steadfast hope, where year after year a tree of sorts, together with an array of green and a splash of colorful flowers, dismissed the description of their locale defiantly, and flourished, except when it snowed. It was a

Cinderella scene in a setting of soot and cement, where nobody would even dream about an invitation to the ball. Here in an immigrant enclave in the city of Passaic, in a cold-water flat directly above a quite popular saloon, I grew into early adolescence. I was a sophomore in high school before we moved away.

From the age of six, or maybe seven, I spent most of my free time sitting on the porch of my grandmother's house, which overlooked her garden. I wrote my earliest poems there, lost in a world a world away from the space that I inhabited. As soon as I got home from school, I would ride the currents of my imagination to the planet's edge and beyond. It was a sacred place. I matured there theologically, although I would not have understood what this meant at that time.

My grandparents were Protestant. The rest of us were Catholic, for my mother had converted. Protestants were destined to burn in hell. That's the way it was back then. We never talked about it. On Sunday mornings, when we were in church and my grandfather was still sleeping, my grandma would go behind the bar, slip two large bottles of soda — birch beer and cream soda — into a brown paper bag, hide it under her apron, tiptoe up the flight of stairs, and leave it outside our door. Now what kind of God would condemn to hell a gentle woman who gave her grandchildren gifts of love from her heart? Certainly not the God I knew. If God could make rainbows and butterflies and a person as good as my grandma and as beautiful as her garden, which she graciously shared with me, then God could surely find a way to let Protestants into heaven. Of this, I had no doubt. I kept these thoughts to myself for a long time after I came of age. Meanwhile, seeds of unconditional love sown in the heart of a little child kept growing and growing and growing, overtaking all.

Years later I went back to the garden, but not the one in New Jersey. I would often revisit the biblical story of Eve in the Garden of Eden, where, they say, everything began. Injustice involving a woman and a garden had remained imprinted on my soul and cried out for restitution, for my grandmother's story and Eve's story, to me, were one and the same. I had come to know the difference between fact and interpretation, and as I wrestled with the text, I realized a shift in meaning would also lead to a different outcome. This would be possible if Eve and her garden were seen through another lens. What if Eve had left Eden with enthusiasm, not regret? How would this affect the role of women who came after?

In recent years many of us have struggled with these questions. How would our lives have been different, how would the world and the church have evolved, if women had been praised, not blamed, for taking the initiative, for wanting to know good from evil, for wanting to be more like God? We might have had peace on earth by now if women had been applauded, rather than berated, for choosing to be fully human, with all that this entailed. Our world is in a mess today because of our inability to distinguish good from evil in so many aspects of our lives.

The Garden story and its application kept women in bondage in body and spirit until feminist scholars helped us reenter and exit the Garden of Eden without the additional baggage and, praise be to God, the guilt. A strong woman and a fruitful tree in the middle of a garden had long been symbolic of female leadership in religion and society before the onslaught of patriarchy wiped it all away.

There is another garden story that has significance here. In that part of the world where the Garden of Eden myth originated, an itinerant teacher staunchly resisted its patriarchal hold. Jesus, man of miracles, and of flesh and blood like the rest of us, was put to death for seeking to move beyond the prevailing paradigm that determined those the system would favor and those it would exclude. There was a garden close to the place where Jesus had been crucified. In it was a tomb that had never been used, and this is where they laid him. The morning after, Mary of Magdala discovered the tomb was empty. She turned to speak to the gardener, but it was not the gardener. There before her was Jesus. Other women also saw him, saw the risen Jesus, saw him in the garden, radiant and transformed. Suddenly, the Garden paradigm shifted, along with the status of women, empowering thcm from within.

Women have always been eyewitnesses to that which society fails to see, which was, and is, Spirit rising from the remnants of defeat. Implicit here are challenges, not only for women, but also for men.

Do not cling to the old ways. Do not be afraid to witness to what you have seen and heard. Let go of power that overpowers and the need to be believed. To be such is sure to catapult us into a parallel universe, for following Jesus necessitates being steeped in paradox, as his teachings often indicate and his actions emphasize.

Blessed are those who are poor, and blessed are those who are persecuted. This is the gospel of Jesus. When things get confrontational, step back and turn the other cheek. Go the distance, and, on arrival, add an extra mile. Pray for those who pick on you. Tolerate the intolerable. Be liberal in your loving. Love even your enemy.

Whoever aspires to be number one will have to begin at the end of the line. Whoever wants to be a leader will have to be willing to serve. If we would be like Jesus, then we need to hang out with people who, according to the prevailing paradigm, do not belong, are undeserving, will never be good enough.

I know a lot of people — Christian, Muslim, Jew, Hindu, Buddhist, Wiccan, and others in diverse social settings and on various spiritual paths — who, like my grandmother, know good from evil, live in ways approved by God, love simply and are simply loving, kind, compassionate, just. This is the new community of faith in our evolving universe, flexible and hospitable, with a vision that is big enough to let anybody in.

Paradox and Praise

Paradoxology integrates paradox and doxology, resulting in a fusion between the unpredictable and praise. Holy are the offspring that come forth from this conjoining. The sacredness of science. The serendipity of sacramentality. A sensuality of the spirit. A presumption of surprise.

Paradox is, quite simply, what is not supposed to happen. It is what you get precisely when you are expecting something else. In the physical world or the world of the spirit, it is the persistent manifestation of a principle we prefer to ignore: God's ways are not our ways.

Doxology means praise, expressed in word or action. "Glory be to the Living God" and "Praise to you, O Holy One" are doxological phrases or doxologies. The Christian doxology is ordinarily Trinitarian. Long before this evolution, however, praise to God our Creator permeated all of life, as reflected in the biblical psalms. Creation, through its very existence, is an ongoing hymn of praise.

A part of me has always understood doxology to be wide open. From the moment I learned to say amen, the world around me and the world within me were manuals for prayer and praise. Even as I became steeped in the paradigmatic ways of my faith tradition and boundaries of legitimate praise became increasingly circumscribed, I continued to celebrate the liturgy of life in a parallel universe in a variety of ways.

It took a series of paradigm shifts in religion and society to liberate my spirit so that I might publicly proclaim that paradoxology is praise of the Divine in a quantum universe, where paradox is paradigm.

Paradoxology permeates life with a unifying spirit, even where paradox interrupts, overturning our expectations, messing up our plans. It is our wave of continuity as we move in and out of a parallel universe created by our longings and filled with kindred spirits, where energy is interchanged in dynamic, chaotic ways.

Paradoxology is eternal. In a quantum universe, past, present, and future are contemporaneously interwoven, so we can look to the past for wisdom while shaping a future pregnant with hope, as we move through a here and now that is coming apart at the seams.

Paradoxology is, quite simply, that which is unceasing: the praise inherent in paradox and the paradox of that praise.

Paradoxology challenges just about everything we take for granted, urging us toward a new way of being and behaving.

Paradoxology is keeping faith when accused of being unfaithful; channeling hope for the hopeless teetering on the brink of despair; loving when love is in short supply and sure to be rejected.

Paradoxology is "thanks be to God" even in the midst of a struggle to divest of our deficiencies.

Paradoxology means forgiving before one has been forgiven and remaining open to finding the appropriate way to reconcile.

Paradoxology means our heart is saturated with divinity, making us totally capable of inviting the whole chaotic world into its embrace.

Paradoxology promises a breakthrough into freedom, primarily freedom from fear: fear of the unknown, fear of what others might think of us, fear of being dishonest or hypocritical or wrong. We no longer have to pretend to understand what is beyond understanding, no longer have to assent to that which violates the soul.

Paradoxology is firmly rooted where we take a stand for justice. Forever after, we will know we were standing on holy ground.

Paradoxology is, above all, uninterrupted praise, the multifaceted energies of all God's creation — past, present, and still to come — echoing amen upon amen to all that is, just as it is, paradoxically. Holy, holy, holy: reverberating, interactive, intergalactic praise.

Chapter 2

The World We Live In,
That Lives In Us

It is said that remnants of our evolving are encoded in our DNA, that a long-forgotten lineage lingers on in our cellular memory and is transmitted in perpetuity from one generation to the next. Was it I who, once upon a time, ran through forests, foraged for food, and drummed and danced in the moonlight? Did I fly through the wind currents effortlessly, once upon a morning star, long, long ago? Is that why my heart skips a beat whenever I hear the flutter of wings on a migratory path in September? Why do I have such a longing to slip into Earth's oceans and seas, rivers and streams in my treks across our planet? Was I, at one time, aquatic? When I rose to the surface, when I came forth, was it I who gathered up the waters and tucked them away inside? Why have I often wondered whether I came to Earth from a neighboring star? Because I feel its fire in my belly? Who am I, then, if I am not the fulfillment of what has been in the past and the promise of whatever will be?

My journey from the seamier side of a city in New Jersey to this day decades later is but a quantum moment riddled with paradox. It might seem like a straight line led me from the votive candles in a darkened church to the doorstep of a convent and fidelity ever after. The path, however, has been far from linear, and unpredictable. The girl who said she would never teach has spent a lifetime teaching, or more accurately, being taught. The decision to embrace a medical mission somewhere overseas, far away from the familiar, took flesh in a series of healing ministries very close to home. Instead of medicine, there was music, and liturgy, and theology, with opportunities to travel, in spirit, anywhere on Earth, and beyond, for no matter where I sojourned, some part of me, deep within, was always moving on.

Wherever I was, even as a child, my world was never big enough, so I turned to what was unfathomable: the night sky and its galaxy of stars, a full moon rising, the rim of a horizon that remained forever beyond my reach, the far side of the planet, and always — all ways — God. To enlarge the circumference of my narrow frame of reference and projection, I stepped out of my taffeta prom dress in the mid-1950s and into a postulant's garb. Then I stepped out of my religious habit in the wake of Vatican II and returned to secular dress, but not to secular ways; sang songs of earthly relevance in the hallowed haunts of religion; entered into the faith experience of other than Catholic Christians ahead of the acceptable time. I became a radical feminist, experienced cross-cultural immersions, established interfaith relationships, embraced ecology and cosmology, and awoke one day to the quantum universe I had been living in all along.

The thread of continuity weaving everything together for me was always an inner urge to write, not complicated pieces, but short, simple expressions of where I am and how I feel and what existence means to me at a particular point in time. Poems from a very early age and, later on, songs and hymns are steeped in imagery I now would call cosmological, and maybe even quantum. Long before I had ever heard the word "cosmology" or been exposed to quantum reality, those forces were at work within, inspiring me and reshaping me for a time such as this. I integrated nature and need and events and spirit and spirituality with biblical themes and daily life and did so with an ease that could only have come from an innate sense that all is connected and that all of us are one.

To speak of a quantum perspective is to put a name to that which has always pulled me beyond my limits into a way of being in the world, a way of perceiving reality, that is far more magnanimous than my setting in life allows. I know there are others who have felt this way, who have struggled within the constraints of religion and society to embrace the call of the Spirit unconditionally. This sense of searching for something more is characteristic of a lot of us who have come through the wars, both literally and figuratively, and no longer want to be against anything or anyone anymore. The disconnect we feel inside is the call of an ancient wisdom whispering, Come home to who you really are, traveler from the everlasting hills, blessed and embodied spirit. Do not be afraid to dream big dreams, to reach beyond the immediate, to rejoice in the sacred that appears everywhere in all manner of guises. We are quantum spirits, we who have breath and being. We are held as we were, and as we are, in God's eternal now, in the palm of our Creator's life-giving, loving hand.

We can hardly accept the premise that we are quantum beings living paradoxically in a quantum world situated in a quantum universe without knowing something about this increasingly prolific term.

"Quantum" means, literally, a specific amount, and in physics, the whole amount of a unit of energy in the subatomic realm. "Quanta," the plural form of "quantum," means chunk of energy, again, the whole amount. Everything in existence consists of those chunks of energy scientists call quanta — too small to be seen, too swift to be captured, too numerous to even imagine. All those angels we used to say could fit on the head of a pin pale in comparison to the astronomical number of quanta inside a single cell underneath the tip of our finger. Quanta give form and substance to the reality that we are.

Those dynamic chunks of energy are constantly in motion. Mechanics is the study of motion, and quantum mechanics is the study of energy in motion, of quanta, the stuff of life. The terrain of quantum mechanics has been the world of the infinitesimally small, where nothing can be seen directly but a lot can be discerned; and because of the nature of our physical world, its scope necessarily extends throughout the infinitely large expanse of our known universe and to everything in between.

Quantum theory's focus has been the fundamental elements of nature within the atom. The existence of the atom — the word means "indivisible" — can be traced back to Democritus, a philosopher in ancient Greece. He conceptualized that these invisible entities are the building blocks of nature. Classical physicists of the nineteenth century conceived of atoms as particles similar to billiard balls whose action was predictable, but when quantum physicists began their atomic and subatomic explorations to verify this assumption, that is not what they found.

What had been a point of absolute certitude was proven to be otherwise and had to be reconceived.

As scientists dug deeper, they discovered ever smaller elements existing within the atom. The electron became the focal point of early quantum research. Although no one had ever seen an electron, and, after a century of observation, it seems no one ever has, it formed the basis of their conjectures and eventually their conclusions.

There is common ground here between science and spirituality. Both have spoken definitively about what is observed only indirectly through its effects. While science points to empirical evidence to substantiate its claims, spirituality relies on its faith traditions, and these have been reluctant to reconsider or to question what has always been said to be so. Spirituality understands that there are fundamental imperatives one simply has to accept on faith, but there are also a significant number of culturally conditioned accretions that are either no longer relevant or else are characteristic of realities that are diverse. Science has given us a new and more enlightened understanding of our physical world. Spirituality in this quantum universe enters the conversation eager to contribute and open to change.

Scientific experiments that shattered the veneer of certainty are also fertile ground for nonscientific reflection. We begin with this consideration. Early efforts to determine both the location and the path of a single electron led to the discovery that it is impossible to know a subatomic particle's position and its movement at precisely the same time. This surprising development regarding a fundamental element of matter was the beginning of the end of how we understood the world in which we live. It is known as the principle of uncertainty. To know where something is and not be able to determine where it will go or where it has come from has scientific implications most of us will not understand. Analogously, however, there is potential here for learning more about life and for reshaping spirituality.

We are so accustomed to knowing both location and locomotion that it is a genuine effort to separate the two. I sit at my desk, and then I get up and go over to my computer, or pour a cup of coffee, or leave the house for a walk. I know exactly where I am, where I have been, and where I intend to be going. Prior to taking a trip by car, I print out a set of directions that outline, step by step, the route to my destination. Again, I am cognizant of what is before, during, and after all along the way. Life itself is a journey. We can map where we are and where we were and where we hope to be going, physically and philosophically, for we are always on our way to somewhere from wherever we have just been.

This reflects a basic orientation within our physical world. At any given time, we live suspended between the past and the future. The present is influenced by what has occurred or by what lies ahead. The winding path we have stumbled along is prelude to every bend in the road. Our hopes, dreams, resolutions, and goals, historic events, and collective wisdom impact our decisions as we opt for this or that. Most of the time, most of us seem to know exactly where things are or where we think they should be, even when it comes to the intangible and unseen. We think we know where heaven is and precisely who will be there; we can name those places where the Divine most certainly abides. We are sure we know what it will take to arrive at our destination, which is eternal bliss, conveniently ignoring this caveat: "No one knows the mind of God." Or the preferences. Or the love. Unpredictable, all-encompassing love.

Science offers a sobering note. Whatever is visible and tangible, and that includes the likes of us, is made up of matter we cannot see, of elements wildly and unpredictably different from anything we have experienced or can even begin to imagine. How does this subatomic aspect, in us and in everything, affect the world that we perceive? What does it tell us about ourselves, our reality, our destiny? About the past and the future? About innovation and tradition? About transition and the temporality of time?

If what we cannot see has an impact on our daily lives, then who are we really? If it is impossible to know the next step before we make a move, if where we are going will be revealed while we are on the journey, if that is part of who we are, why so many restrictions that impede the flow of grace? And why are we so reluctant to simply go with the flow? Why do we insist that manmade rules and regulations are essential to map the way? Billions of chunks of energy move with breakneck speed within us and everywhere around us, now here, now there, neither here nor there, perpetually in motion, as we kneel before our icons and whisper our amen. To predetermine the appropriate path seems out of synch with reality. Perhaps that is why we are not always sure of exactly where we are going. Maybe it is enough, sometimes, simply to be where we are.

Here is another discovery that impacts the life of the spirit. In brief, in quantum physics, the path or the position of a subatomic particle comes into existence only when it is observed. This conclusion has ignited a spirited debate that continues to this day. It redefines the role of the observer in what is being observed, making observation constitutive of what is revealed. According to quantum theory, the way an experiment is arranged predetermines its outcome. If one sets out to observe a particle's location, one learns where the particle is. If one seeks to measure its movement, the data reveal that result. Subatomic elements manifest only what is asked of them, never otherwise.

Think about this for a moment. Quantum physics tells us that we actively participate in creating what we see. Some physicists say the world exists only because we are looking at it. Physical reality is a phenomenon. Manifestation of the physical world is contingent on being seen. Many within the scientific community and a lot of us out here in the trenches do not necessarily agree with this, but before we relegate this point of view to the realm of science fiction, we need to understand that the relationship of observation and actualization is serious quantumstuff.[4] Implications involve reality. What is the meaning of reality? What is really real? Is there an "out there" out there? These questions linger, which is why quantum theory is so difficult to understand. Most responses are not quantum facts but quantum interpretation. There is broad-based consensus concerning the facts of quantum physics, but a lot of disagreement regarding what those facts might mean. Since this remains an ongoing debate, it is vitally important that we who bring a faith perspective to our interpretations and our applications step up and have our say. If science can give to humanity the awesome power of creating a world with an act of observation, then spirituality can give it right back to the Source, where it belongs.

This we know for certain. The role of the observer is undergoing significant change. On some level we no longer are disengaged spectators who look at the world from the sidelines and passively accept what we see. More and more we are asking penetrating questions about life on our planet. This may be the way it is, but is it the way it has to be? How can we make a difference? What can we do to initiate change if we don't like what we see? On the other hand, colloquial wisdom says that we only see what we want to see. How often do we look at something and never really see it? How easy it is to miss the signs that have been there all along. We find only what we are looking for. That particular adage really resonates with me. I remember asking, years ago, why were there so few biblical women that anyone ever spoke about, and I was told there really weren't very many women to speak of in the Bible. So I went looking for them, and they showed up in droves, eager to tell their stories to me and to many others.

In some sense we do create the reality around us. The path to peace comes into existence when we make it happen. A broken relationship is healed because, by envisioning the outcome, we help bring it about. A pioneering feminist principle says that we hear one another into speech.[5] Quantum mechanics seems to say that we see one another into life. To a little child, being seen delivers validation. "Look at me, Mommy, look at me," and a bundle of energy erupts to energize us all. So many people, young and old, realize their potential through the eyes of love.

I see goodness in someone who is deemed incorrigible, and because I see it, goodness begins to make its presence known. Again and again the power of love makes something or someone real. We can start a chain reaction by activating, through observation, those minuscule chunks of loving energy that proliferate everywhere.

Another finding in the field of physics is particularly intriguing. It concerns particles and waves. It had been understood that the constituent elements of matter were either particle or wave, until quantum scientists concluded that fundamental elements are both particle and wave. The initial reaction was, how is this possible? How can an element subsist simultaneously as both particle and wave? A particle has substance. A wave does not. A particle can have location. A wave cannot, for a wave is a wave of motion, or movement, or momentum. One or the other, common sense insists, yet the fundamental elements of all that exists are not either/or but both/and, both substantive and without substance, both particle and wave. An object's wave and particle behavior mutually exclude each other, yet both are necessary. Subatomic units of matter have this dual aspect. Their appearance as either particles or waves depends on how we look at them. Once again it is the observer who has the decisive say.

As I continue to reflect on this, a mischievous musical phrase keeps messing with my mind. "Sometimes you feel like a wave. Sometimes you don't." That about sums it up for me. There are times when all of us feel the energy radiating from within us and anything seems possible. Then there are times when we just go splat, as the wave that seemed to carry us along suddenly runs out of steam. A collapse of the wave function allows the particle to come to the fore. So says quantum theory. I sense some innate wisdom here, but I suspect it will be a while before it finds its way into words.

We conclude this glimpse of quantumstuff with a behavior issue in the microcosmic realm. An electron does not move in a continuous, flowing manner, but jumps discontinuously from one orbit to another. This is the origin of the proverbial "quantum leap." It really spooked the observers. This was not what they had predicted, those theoreticians who hypothesized how particles moved from here to there. They expected some kind of continuity, some sense of orbital flow. Observation revealed that electrons jumped back and forth between orbits within the atom. Try to imagine warp speed and speeds considerably faster, not circling around or spiraling around, but in capricious motion, an avalanche of particles engaged in discontinuous leaps to orbital positions resulting in an implicate order not necessarily preordained according to some primordial plan. Millions of them. Billions of them. Trillions, yes, trillions of them. The fundamental stuff of matter. Erratic. Sporadic. Unpredictable. Another theoretical assumption moves a hop, skip, and a jump away from empirical validation, because what had been concluded before had never been that way.

I like the phrase "quantum leap." It is something I can relate to. It was, for me, a metaphor wide open to application long before I was introduced to the origins of the term. I am constantly shifting orbits, leaping precariously close to the edge, making outrageous associations before I connect the dots. And yes, there is frenetic activity when deadlines coincide. There but for the grace of God might I go spinning out of control, leaping frantically to and fro between unfulfilled expectations with too much to do in too little time.

Quantum leap. More than metaphor. It is integral to us. It is the reality inside of us, where a universe of activity occurs in every cell of our body every moment of every day. I think about that mysterious realm whenever I am feeling stressed, when I try to keep from jumping to conclusions that do not have a basis in fact. Leaping, jumping electrons are the very substance of who I am. Therefore, cellmates, I say to you, enjoy your slapstick behavior, while I access the source of restorative stillness that also bubbles up within. Then, when I hear the music of the celestial spheres, I'll join you in the dancing, an image many quantum enthusiasts associate with quantum leaps.

Quantum mechanics has revealed to us aspects of our physical world we could never have imagined solely on our own. We have stood at the very threshold of the universe of the atom, felt its boundless energy, hidden from our eyes. All that is or ever was can be traced back to that invisible, subatomic configuration, to the atom and its nucleus and its vast array of particles and related particle species: photons, electrons, protons, neutrons, mesons, leptons, quarks, literally hundreds of subatomic elements, each with different properties and distinguishing characteristics, moving in and out of existence, unlimited and unceasing.

I found quantum physics impossible to understand and was relieved to discover that aspects of quantum theory remain incomprehensible even to scientists. In the early days of its development, Albert Einstein made this comment: "The more success quantum mechanics has, the sillier it looks."[6] Richard Feynman, a contemporary physicist, says: "I think it is safe to say that no one understands quantum mechanics."[7] Fred Alan Wolf, who has written many books on quantum physics, adds: "Quantum theory is correct, and it is as weird as ever."[8] Whether or not it makes sense to us, we are now living in a quantum world. Therefore, quantum reality is presented here as the basis for shaping spirituality in a quantum universe.

Science and spirituality share common ground. Both wrestle with a reality that surpasses understanding. Both pledge allegiance to what can be seen only through its effects. All my life I have been faithful to an ultimate imperative that is beyond comprehension, a reality seen only indirectly through its manifestations; yet my commitment to the unknown continues to make sense to me. I have always been drawn to mystery, aware that wisdom is not the result of logical conclusions. Only recently have I discovered that this is an orientation scientists also share.

Proponents of quantum mechanics and of spirituality have a passion for the physical world, for nature and its origins and what it means to exist. They are engaged in both the physical and the metaphysical, but with starkly different starting points and vastly different outcomes. Both, believe it or not, value imagination. Einstein, whose theoretical brilliance gave rise to quantum physics, is said to have said: "Logic will get you from A to B. Imagination will take you anywhere."[9] Imagination is what one turns to in order to fill the void and, in the process, bring to birth new visions and new vistas. Imagination, for poet and mystic, toddler and saint, and yes, for theoretician, is essential for discovery and the kind of creativity that takes us by surprise, for without imagination, there would be no quantum leap. For these and many other reasons, I am convinced of the necessity of learning to look at the world we live in through a quantum lens.

Quantum theory's weird and wondrous contribution to human knowledge offers a solid basis for constructing a spirituality rooted in this world, this resilient, remarkable world, with all its dynamic differentiation and propensity for change. Spirituality in a quantum universe is uniquely oriented toward an emerging global society that fosters a collective desire for peace within neighborhoods and among nations. As we look to the far horizons of our universe, and beyond, as we probe the microcosmically minute realities within all that is, as we mix and mingle with cultures characteristically different from our own, we are moved to set our certainties aside, to temper our expectations, and, in time, to restructure our praise.

Location and motion, particle and wave, observation and actualization, discontinuity and stability, chaos and order, and energy: this is just the beginning. Spirituality has a lot to contribute to the conversation on quantum-stuff: perspectives on reality and meaning; on having a sense of assurance in a world that is in flux; on actualizing what is potentially there and is said to be impossible; on ubiquitous energy; and on how the universe can be perceived as integrated wholeness, where all within are one. Physics and spirituality need to take the next step together, for the wisdom of our separate disciplines is incomplete on its own.

In the following pages, aspects of quantum theory will serve as a springboard for deepening our awareness of the interconnectedness, perhaps more accurately stated as the innerconnectedness, of seemingly disparate realities: the physical and the spiritual, large and small, far and near, tactile and ephemeral, as reflected in life on our planet and its spatial environment. The purpose of this is to broaden the scope of what can be said to be sacred and to consider how we might perceive the Divine as enveloping all. Adding intentionality to this substratum of insight will reveal how a spirituality in synch with a quantum universe is within our reach.

Let go
of the need
to be secure,
of the urge to be
absolutely sure,
the luxury
of certainty,
as if
"as it were"
could ever be.
Worlds
within worlds
within subatomic entities,
worlds
beyond worlds,
galactic immensities,
give us a glimpse,
though never enough,
of quantum connectedness
and quantumstuff.

The mystery
we cannot see
in hidden fields
of energy,
that sumptuous
reality:
tantalizing, terrifying, mystifying, mesmerizing,
enticing us
to the very edge
of forever and ever.
Jump!

Part Two

Quantum Leap

Chapter 3

The Divine Milieu

Long, long ago...oh, so very long ago...before memory and meaning...before being and becoming...before what if? when will? why not? Long, long before the articulation "in the beginning...." Can you even imagine? Before there was light that made sense of the dark. Before there was anything to signify something. Before "after." Before "before." More than a billion years ago (time is our way of conceiving). More than ten billion years ago. More or less fifteen billion years ago our own history began. But that is not where the story starts. That is the beginning of *our* story, which is a minuscule moment within a context so much greater than our cosmological setting.

The story within which our own unfolds is the story of the living God. A story with no beginning or end. No details to fill in the blanks before our own genealogies originate. No facts. No speculations. Except the initial assumption that such a story was and is. It can be intuited only through faith. And imagination. Try to imagine "forever and ever" prior to "in the beginning," prior to fifteen billion years ago. Devoid of physicality, sensuality, spirituality. Filled with Essence. Existence. Presence. Being. Divinity. God.

In the beginning,
whenever that was:
a flaring forth,
whatever that means:
out of the depths and into light
ENERGY
erupting
exploding
expelling
ENERGY
expanding, emerging, evolving
as cosmic entities evolved
as everything on planet Earth has evolved
as you and I even now are evolving
ENERGY
permeating, penetrating, predicating
the Divine Milieu
DIVINITY
spilling over into
visibility and viability
photons of light
particle and wave
eternally becoming
whatever was, is, will be
Matrix of reality
in Whom we live
in Whom we move
in Whom we have our being.

At the beginning of our wider world, a cosmic mael-
strom strewn across a seemingly endless expanse of space
...fireballs and gaseous clouds...comets, suns, stars,

moons, asteroids, and planets . . . a turbulent mix of galaxies and dark holes and enormous stretches of invisible energy reaching into infinity . . . imagine, out of this cosmic chaos, seven billion years ago, the beginning of our more immediate world, planet Earth, emerging.

Inhospitable at first, yet after perhaps half a billion years, that which we call home came alive. This cosmic blip burgeoned with fertility, becoming an eco-friendly oasis, productive and prolific. Imagine Divinity shepherding its growth through every stage of development, innately and incarnately, not from without but from within, as wave of abiding love. If this were how we saw creation — and this is how I see it — then we would have to radically reorient the way we look at life, the way we relate to the living, and the way we speak about God.

Throughout Earth's evolution, as we who are more than matter sought stability and sustainability, as generation after generation found its vitality and voice, we paid homage to the Ground of our Being, albeit in diverse ways. The origins of humanity go all the way back five million years to the beginning of our evolving, but our unique way of being human is far more recent than that.

Homo sapiens has been around for approximately one hundred thousand years, and we can trace its ancestry back for a similar length of time. What is that when compared to the billions of eons that preexisted us? The human species is a microsecond in our cosmic story, yet we act as though we know it all as we speak of God, speak to God, and even speak for God. In the short span of our religious lives, approximately seven thousand years, we removed God from the midst of us and decisively from within us. We have relegated divinity to scripted rites and sacred sites, to mountain peak and lingering cloud, to shrines and sanctuaries, to tabernacles and temples, and limited incarnations.

When I was a child preparing for my First Holy Communion, I had to memorize questions and answers from the *Baltimore Catechism*, which was the authoritative theological source for Catholics at that time. "Where is God?" It was my mother who first posed the question to me as we rehearsed what I had to know. The seven-year-old within me still feels a surge of the Spirit whenever I respond. "God is everywhere." Where? Everywhere! Shout it from the rooftops. Tell it to your friends. God is everywhere. And where is everywhere? It is *everywhere.* We hardly hear anything anymore about the ubiquity of God, about the *everywhereness* of God. At the core of the teachings of Christianity, and of other faiths as well, is the conviction that God is everywhere. This premise, long buried beneath a religious rigidity, is genuinely quantum. I am still learning to take it literally and to live accordingly in God's eternal now. Sometimes, I just want to sing:

> God is everywhere, with us on the run:
> verily, verily, verily, verily, loving everyone.[10]

There have always been those who have known life to be reflected Being, who see the sacred in the physical world and live in awe at the privilege of standing on holy ground. Most people, however, have a hard time with the concept of Divinity everywhere. There has to be a more dignified way of engaging with transcendence, or so we have believed. Better to know God is here or there and available on demand. We need to have some psychic space to be free to do what we want to do without being reminded by everything everywhere that here and now is not all there is. That may be why we continue to separate sacred and profane. Besides, it is only natural that everything is located somewhere. Even God. Especially God. But where, if not right here?

Up. Down. Without. Within. Near at hand or far away. Spiritually, God may remain close. Theologically, if God gets too close, we tend to push God away. Far too often, when we pray, we send our prayers aloft. There is still the prevailing perception that God is somewhere out there, beyond the range of our explorations, yet always within our reach. God is up in heaven, many among the faithful insist, yet precisely where is that? Once we leave the planet, any which way is up. To lift off from planet Earth as some anticipate on that day when the final trumpet sounds means people ascending in all directions, never to arrive in any one place, never to meet again. This may appear to be pushing a metaphor well beyond its limits, but it is an authentic image borrowed from Australian author Michael Morewood, whose "up" Down Under clearly substantiates this speculation. Besides, the rotation of our planet ensures that "up" is a concept that is perennially in flux.

Envisioning God as apart from us belongs to a past paradigm, one that separates and segregates in every kind of way. We live in an interconnected world, one that constantly challenges the isolationist mentality dominant in the past. Divinity permeates the world we inhabit. God is in the world, and the world is in God, guiding us from within. Teilhard de Chardin knew this as he wrote of the divine milieu:

For me, my God, all joy and all achievement, the very purpose of my being and all my love of life, all depend on this one basic vision of the union between yourself and the universe.[11]

How is it possible, some will ask, to meld finite and infinite? This is blasphemy. How, I cannot answer. In fact, nobody can, for the ways of God are not our ways and the mind of God is infinitely beyond our comprehension. This much I can contribute. God is always God, and matter is always matter, yet infused somehow, and in some way, with divinity, from the subatomic particle to the farthest frontiers of outer space. This does not limit the Divine nor imply that what has been created is coterminous with Creator, for when we come to the very end of all that has been created, God, infinite Creator, continues infinitely on. In the realm of spirituality, one does not always have the answers, yet can live in peace with the questions and some interim assumptions. Here intuition, imagination, and inspiration are fluid enough and generous enough to support ambiguity. As we have seen, science does not have all the answers either. There isn't a whole lot of difference between a quantum leap and a leap of faith.

From a faith perspective, this interrelationship between divinity and matter reflects a major paradigm shift, but not a new addition. Symbols of the sacred in the natural world of our ancestors hint of some inherent connection understood even then. There are and always have been two interpretive streams flowing through biblical tradition and through many of those religious and spiritual traditions with the Bible as their source. One is theologically based and the other is mystical. Mystics from many faith traditions envisioned and often experienced how the

Divine and that which the Divine creates are essentially intertwined. For Christians the divine and human realms have been bridged in the person of Jesus and the doctrine of Incarnation. Otherwise, the dominant teaching of Christianity today, as it has been for centuries, holds to a strict separation between God and God's creation. Occasionally, someone breaks the mold among authoritative voices. For example, Gregory of Nyssa, a fourth-century theologian and bishop.

> When one considers the universe, can anyone be so simple-minded as not to believe that the Divine is present in everything, pervading, embracing and penetrating it?[12]

These are the words of a mystic. The mystical stream, a free-flowing source of wisdom and understanding, often spills over efforts to contain it, seeping into cracks and crevices on both sides of any wall.

Before the primacy of theology, which seeks an understanding of God, trumped theophany, which is an experience of God, personal encounters with the Divine were a primary source of theological reflection and integral to the everyday lives of ordinary people. The Bible is full of stories in which individuals and communities interact with God with an immediacy and familiarity that make one long to resurrect the spirit of those times. Then a divine encounter often resulted in giving God a name. When God visited a vulnerable Hagar out in the wilderness, she called the One who reached out to her El-roi, "the God who sees." Shaddai, one with breasts; Shekinah, indwelling presence; Sophia, divine wisdom:

these female God-images and names are integral to biblical tradition, the result of mystical experiences with the Divine.[13]

All such images and names were imagined, once upon a time. Rising Sun, Living Water, Bread of Life, Morning Star — from the beginning of civilization, the Divine has been seen metaphorically in some aspect of creation and reflected back to us in fragments, thereby bestowing on the natural world sacramental potency. In the twelfth century Hildegard of Bingen heard the divine Creator speaking from the heart of creation:

> I am that supreme and fiery force that sends forth all the sparks of life. I shine in the water, I burn in the sun and the moon and the stars. Mine is the mysterious force of the invisible wind. I sustain the breath of all that lives. I, the fiery power, lie hidden in these things and they blaze forth from me.[14]

A century later another mystic, Meister Eckhart, wrote: "God created all things in such a way that they are not outside God. All creatures remain within God...enveloped by God." [15] Prophetic voices through the ages, indigenous voices, mystical voices from many religious and cultural traditions, witness to a divine presence permeating all. Their experience is replicated in ordinary people living ordinary lives. Even today we hear divine wisdom whispering everywhere.

> I am the rays of the rising sun,
> snow on the Mountains of the Moon,
> the far-flung canopy of stars,
> the shadows of late afternoon.

I am the wisdom of the sage.
I am the refuge of all who weep.
I am the mother of all who live.
I am the promises I keep.

I am the one who sits with sorrow.
I am the one who feels your pain.
I am the hope of your tomorrow.
I am the one who will remain.[16]

Our sacred stories tell of a God who is very close to us —
like a mother's womb, like the air we breathe, like the beat-
ing of our hearts. More often than we dare acknowledge,
many of us have experienced God in intimate and transformative ways, and we are no longer willing or able to keep
this good news to ourselves. As Western spirituality begins
once again to emphasize immanence, those images and
names, metaphors and rituals that reflect this theologically
are already commonplace, helping us transcend what seems
like an ontological distance between creation and Creator
by providing sacramental bridges, conduits to and from the
Divine, channeling multifaceted aspects of divinity.

God-images change as times change, and even as we
change. Christianity has outgrown that familiar God-
image of an aging patriarch presiding over heaven and
keeping tabs on Earth. In this age of cosmological awareness, we now acknowledge and gratefully celebrate the
cosmos as the embodiment of God. It is "a plausible
theological response" to contemporary science, says Sallie
McFague, author of *The Body of God*,[17] and a satisfying
ecological response to the steadily growing numbers determined to save a beleaguered planet. The images and
names I have had for God are markers on my spiritual

journey that reflect a theological evolution through layer
after layer of an inner unfolding, preparing the way for cosmic wisdom in a quantum universe. Even though these
are no longer needed, they continue to be a blessing when
wedded to poetry and song.

Underneath the shifting surface of our quantum universe lies our Rock of Ages and the human heart's insatiable hunger to hook up with its Maker in its own
inimitable way. Knowing and naming God is a person's
fundamental right, as unique as love between lovers, as
basic as human need. When it comes to a tryst with
Divinity, all are potentially mystics, recipients of revelations that none other is privy to. Many of us are listening
to that still, small voice within us and beginning to share
with others what we have seen and heard. For some
time now we have dared to imagine and re-imagine the
Divine in the spirit of our ancestors, cherishing those
opportunities for intimacy with God.

Yes, there is but one divine source, whom many of us
call God, with as many images and names that humanity
can handle, with a love large enough to encompass everything that has been and will be created, and with enough
avenues and paths to accommodate us all. The more multifaceted our awareness, the better we will understand that
we simply cannot understand it, but can embrace it anyway. The Divine is everywhere, within us and around us,
revealing to us through ordinary things the ubiquity of
God. Teilhard de Chardin said it best in his book *The
Divine Milieu.* "Let us leave the surface, and, without
leaving the world, plunge into God."[18]

Take the plunge, into God, into a world teeming with
need and suppressed divinity. Soak it in, surface, then dive

again, dive deep, into the heart of the divine milieu and release unconditional love. There are so many out there, bobbing along, cut loose from their moorings, with no sure star to guide them, no harbor to call their home. There are so many opportunities to keep this sacred planet from suffering debilitating loss. The sea, the sky, forests and fields, glaciers and equators, and every acre in between are sacramental landscapes that serve as the playground of God. These have all been entrusted to us. As caretakers we have to do more than simply take off our sandals. We need to do whatever is necessary to preserve this holy ground. Once more, Teilhard de Chardin:

> All around us, to right and left, in front and behind, above and below, we have only had to go a little beyond the frontier of sensible appearances in order to see the divine welling up and showing through. But it is not only close to us, in front of us, that the divine Presence has revealed itself. It has sprung up so universally, and we find ourselves so surrounded and transfixed by it, that there is no room left to fall down and adore it, even within ourselves. By means of all created things, without exception, the divine assails us, penetrates us and moulds us. We imagined it as distant and inaccessible, whereas in fact we live steeped in its burning layers.[19]

This divine all-encompassing milieu is dynamic, chaotic energy, creating and re-creating, continually giving impetus to that which is beyond anything we can ever imagine. This ever-expanding, life-giving, death-into-life reality is the context of our being and becoming, from which everything emerges and to which all will return.

Divine power, divine presence, divine potentiality can never be contained within the restrictions of rationality, the boundaries of religion, the limitations of law. How can one impose a framework on that which has no beginning and will never come to an end? We who long to live fully and faithfully in a quantum universe firmly believe that God is at the heart of all that is and was and eventually will be and, in some way, is one with our own being and becoming.

In You, O God, we live and move
and have eternal being,
one with all that is:
how wonderfully wise and freeing.

In You the cosmic dream expands,
unfathomed and unending,
to and through the stars
the path of our own transcending.

In You the dance of love is linked
to bonds no one can sever,
reaching out to all
and spiraling on forever.

In You the gift of planet Earth
is sacramental blessing,
Your incarnate mode
abundantly Self-expressing.

Web of Life, woven of soul and sinew.
Web of Life, everything lives within You.

Web of Life, woven of soul and sinew.
Web of Life, everything lives, everything moves,
everything is within You.[20]

Chapter 4

The Sacred Story

It is, after all, God's story, even though we who are human were given the means to put it into words. The results of our loquaciousness fill libraries all over the world and record a trail of memories all the way back to the long-forgotten tales the ancients told. It may seem arrogant for anyone to try to tell the story that only God can tell, but somebody had to do it, and once upon a time, everybody did. How else could one be certain that the story was complete? The campfire, the family meal, the ritual gatherings of the tribe, these were the sacred circles. Life, and all that this implied, was the text of the living word. Underlying local lore and those entertaining tales we continue to tell is a blueprint of who we really are.

We are not people of the book.
We are people of the story.

What lies between the covers of a book can only be a chapter in the ongoing story of Eternal Being that remains forever unfinished, for the living word means living the word and remaining open to new revelations unto eternity. We who live the story are the ones who tell the story and who sometimes write it down. When that story is retold to us, it is so we can reflect upon it, add to it, improvise or re-imagine it, retell it, and then tell it again in order to deepen our understanding or revisit lessons learned from our successes and our mistakes.

Long, long after storytelling eras flourished all over planet Earth, there came a time when free expression was no longer free. Within certain religious circles, only the duly ordained were allowed to speak to and for tradition. Why would anyone need permission to proclaim and to interpret the wonderful works of God? The answer to that is painfully clear: because we are no longer unconditionally Spirit-led. When Scripture locks the story securely onto a printed page, and when the past is canonized in ways that disregard the present to predetermine the future's path, God's story begins to look like something scripted by us.

God's living word is revealed in every facet of creation, and the story is told through all the twists and turns of life's evolving. God's cosmological epic consists of the universe story, planet Earth's story, humanity's story, and our personal stories. Here, in the midst of life unfolding, is the primary source of Revelation. All else, oral and written, is secondary source.

Something vital is missing from the way we relate our foundational myths. It is that ancient wisdom inherent in the natural world that we are only now rediscovering and have not fully understood. As our cosmological awareness expands with images of distant galaxies and newly discovered planets, we realize that our frame of reference is so much more immense than we could have ever imagined, expanding in all directions, seemingly into infinity. Who can say what lies beyond or if ours is the only planet that has been blessed with life? What elements of our story, as a planet and its people, will we have to reconsider in light of all the new information returning from outer space? Scientific discoveries challenge some of our traditional images and associated assumptions, pressing us to improvise contemporary connections interwoven with ancient themes.

How different this feels from the usual way we talk about "in the beginning." So how might we rephrase the myth if we were to begin again? Surely we would start with the flaring forth of the divine milieu and the unfolding of a universe perpetually expanding, the billions of years preparatory to the emergence of a fertile orb warmed by a neighboring sun. We have to start big with a wide-angle lens to introduce perspective, evoke a feeling of breathtaking awe at the immensity of it all and at the billions of years it took before we entered the picture, and then move in much closer to home to focus on the details. If we tell the story as we always have, by taking our cues from a printed page, we confine an infinite wonder to the limits of a literary framework and run the risk that whatever comes after will be narrowly understood as well.

However we choose to tell it, we need to remember that no one really knows what happened back in the beginning because no one was there when nothing was there. Science has given some factual basis to speculation on our origins, and faith fires our imagination to contribute a philosophical frame. With that, we are free to imagine, and for those of us who opt to remain congruent with the Bible, we might say something like this.

In the beginning of our beginning, which is the beginning of planet Earth, there was a differentiating from all else in the universe. Energy fields, particles and waves, molecular configurations on a particular planet evolved to the brink of probability and took a quantum leap into life.

It still remains a mystery, that serendipitous transformation. No matter how many times or ways our creation myths address it or theology tries to explain it, we cannot understand it. Genesis says that Divinity stirred, and out of the dark and formless void, all life ensued. I can live with that.

Metaphorically speaking, which is necessarily the language of all creation myths, there are two catechetical points colloquially expressed in this initial creation story. The first: out of nothing, something. The second: God played a role in whatever occurred, initiating and somehow sustaining its subsequent evolving. The integrating motifs here are the ubiquity of Divinity and the oneness of all creation. This seems to be what they were trying to say in the beginning of biblical tradition, before there was a Bible. Like a mantra, this perspective echoes throughout the book that put an end to the oral and more spontaneous phase of tradition, a time when anyone and everyone could tell it like it is. The Divine is right here with us, inspiring us, sustaining us, acting in and through us in the midst of our daily lives. That is the core biblical word, on and off the page.

How did people know that life is the primary source of revelation? There was nothing else to turn to. For better and for worse, such is the good news of the Bible: that ordinary people living ordinary lives are given extraordinary insight into the meaning of this world and a world beyond it; that we are all recipients of divine inspiration and bits of divine revelation; that the canon of graced experience can never be closed as long as there is life and as long as God is with us, which brings us to forever. Jesus gave this good news flesh and lived and died defending it against a rigid mind-set similar to our own.

Biblical stories were ordinary stories, similar to our stories, in the oral phase of tradition. Some lived on as archetypal examples of God-with-us and circulated freely. Most fulfilled their purpose at the time of their telling and were never heard again. That doesn't mean they are gone forever. Our stories, like our spirits, are absorbed into that energy stream that constitutes creation's cosmic consciousness and are lovingly preserved in God's eternal now. Biblical narratives invite us in to share their inherent wisdom in a way that makes us want to take another look at ourselves. At some point we need to close the book and enter into the story, for this is where we will eventually find a connection to our own.

The key to understanding any story may lie in what was omitted, which is often the backstory, or context. Where, when, why, and any number of extenuating circumstances and their implications impact plot and plausibility more than we realize. This story within a story is the story behind the story and includes other stories the present storytelling reminds us of that we may or may not tell. I often interrupt my "Guess what happened to me today" when another story pops into my mind, because I sense a connection. Such narrative embellishments are not necessarily diversions. These often contextualize a narrative and give it breadth and depth.

The backstory is essential to biblical stories that have been taken out of context and now circulate on their own, for instance, the story of Moses and the burning bush. We miss some of its meaning and relevant applications when we fail to include the stories of all those courageous women who stepped across the dividing lines of race, culture, and class to make it possible for Moses to grow up to liberate his people. The God whose revelation to Moses was, "I will be who I will be," or more simply said, "I Am," is the God of Shiprah and Puah and all the Hebrew midwives, of Jochebed and Miriam, the mother and sister of Moses, of Pharaoh's daughter, who adopted Moses, and of her conspiring handmaids, and of Zipporah, the Midianite, whom Moses would later marry. The Divine One in the wilderness, God of the Hebrews and the Egyptians, is God of all the nations. That revelation would force Moses to come to grips with his own multifaceted and multicultural identity before embracing the call to liberate his people from his people. If only our own multiracial and interreligious situations could receive a divine encounter in the wilderness of our unknowing that would prevent our rushing to war when we might accomplish more through peace.

Science and the new cosmology confirm the importance of the backstory. The universe story is backstory to the biblical account of creation. Putting the two together reveal how an ancient and familiar myth can authentically be made new. Every story arises out of a context that precedes it. Without some prior knowledge of this larger life behind an individual incident or an event, our perspective can be truncated and is often skewed.

There are many ways to tell a story, even the very same story, as creation myths and fairy tales and the sacred texts of diverse religions make abundantly clear. Every storied fragment is integral to the whole, for it adds to the rich diversity in the epic of humanity, illustrating the imagination of a storytelling God. When we share our experience with others, we also add what we think it means and together explore how and why it might be relevant to others.

Telling our story acknowledges our place within the larger story, and here is precisely where the need for a paradigm shift enters in. What is that larger story that has been circulating around our planet since the day that Earth was born? What is the context in which all our individual and collective narratives appropriately belong? We are just beginning to come to terms with the political implications of Earth's multicultural, multireligious, multifaceted, multidimensional overarching story. There is only one planetary story, but it may be a while before we humans are able to adjust to that. Our global perspective is still refracted through a myopic lens, one that tips economic outcomes decisively in our favor, one that gives our own political processes pride of place, one that accords our faith traditions, and seldom anyone else's, spiritual legitimacy.

The narrative of human experience winds through a cosmic storyline along unscripted paths of evolution and revelation, from "once upon a time" toward "happily ever after." We look to the past for wisdom to encourage and sustain us as we head into a future that we cannot quite envision, no matter how hard we try. Our stories of faith reassure us that should we ever find ourselves at the edge of our endurance, we will be given sufficient strength to be able to carry on. In a quantum universe, there are things we have to hold on to. There are also many other things we simply need to let go. The essentials, however, will always remain, as certain as the return of morning after a long and sleepless night, as comforting as a spring green willow when the snow is gone.

We are in need of so many things as we move into tomorrow. We need another epiphany, linked to an unfamiliar star. We need to remain, without wavering, on an unconventional path, convinced that love can overcome fear, that the road less traveled will reveal to us a new and far more secure way of being in the world.

When we come to that place within ourselves where living justly and peacefully is our top priority, when we realize God favors not only us but all life on our planet, we will be ready to listen to the sages from the East. They have much to teach us.

Once upon a time, their story goes, they came to the end of the world they had known and then kept right on going, without a map and with only a dream kept alive by a lingering star. We know how their story ends — in Christianity's beginning. The spirit of the one they sought and found surely hears and empathizes with the anguish of their descendants, waits patiently to enlighten us, to show us all a different way, to accompany us on a new path that will lead us safely home. Joseph Campbell once said:

> The only myth that is going to be worth thinking about in the immediate future is one that is talking about the planet, not the city, not these people, but the planet, and everybody on it.[21]

So put aside the text for a while. Tell tales instead. Share your lived experience, for we are people of the story who need to hear one another's stories for our own to be complete. Spirituality in a quantum universe is rooted in God's story revealed in and through the universe story, in and through our planet's story, in and through our storied lives.

Part Three

Quantum Spirit

Chapter 5

A New Pentecost

The sound of a whirling wind
fills the house that fear inhabits.
Come, come again, we cry:
break into the cramped rooms
where our hesitant hearts are hiding,
decimate indecisiveness
demolish all self-righteousness
dismantle false securities
rigidities, ideologies
redirect our dependencies
and reconstruct our religious lives,
not from the top down
but from the bottom up,
not from outside in
but from the inside out,
as it was in the beginning
of the tradition in which we stand.
Can you imagine the mess that would make?
No more than the mess we are making now.
No worse than the mess we are in.
Where Spirit is
there is chaos
and a call for implicate order
made manifest through the relentless demands

of divinity
in and around us.
O holy, hallowed Spirit,
reckless as a sudden storm,
comforting as a mother's kiss,
we have felt Your stirring deep within us
so many times,
in so many ways
and staggered beneath Your coerciveness
as You called forth from inexperience
the unexplained and unexpected.
Blow away the accretions
of complacency and indifference
and restore originating energy
and unconditional grace.
Come, now, and let us feel
the freedom
of Your presence
the flaming
of Your passion
the full force
of Your power
to shake and shape body and soul
and heart and mind and spirit
like a fire in the belly
igniting a spark
in our senses and our psyches
compelling us
to tell the world
of all that we have witnessed
and all that we have experienced
even before we find the words

and can only babble
about belonging
about becoming
all-inclusive
all caught up
in the wake of an all-encompassing love
and the chance to begin again.
Spirit of the living God,
You know where to find us
and precisely how to reach us,
engendering Pentecost anew
as You blow to bits
again and again
our precious presuppositions
in order to pave a path
here and now
for a radically new creation
in Spirit and in truth.
Listen! Is that the whir of wings?
Listen! Fire! How it sings.

Energy

In the undifferentiated void, a flash, a flaring forth, a primordial thrust into the vast and never-ending expanse of space, the origins of our universe, and whatever else is out there. Energy: roiling, reeling, writhing. Energy: seething, swirling, caroming chaotically and creatively. Invisible energy. Visceral energy. Vigorous, vital, viable energy. Hovering over and hurling forth, churning within and burning throughout. The Spirit of the living God in the form of energy. In the beginning, Energy. In the beginning, Divinity. In the beginning, God.

> Without any doubt, there is *something* which links material energy and spiritual energy together and makes them a continuity. In the last resort there must *somehow* be but one single energy active in the world.[22]

In the words of Teilhard de Chardin over half a century ago, divinity and energy are inexplicably entwined. However one chooses to tell the story, divine energy was there at the beginning and will be there at the end, continuing on beyond the end throughout eternity. That originating blast of energy in the flaring forth of the cosmos is with us everywhere as the air we breathe, the fire within, the life force of our being and our serendipitous becoming. It is the Holy Spirit, of the essence of Divinity, matrix of our reality, an energy spiraling inside and out from the far rim of our universe and all that lies beyond it, to the inner realm of an unseen world as real as real can be.

Biblical tradition takes for granted that the Spirit of God permeates and energizes life. Substitute "energy" for "Spirit" in the Hebrew and Christian scriptures and this becomes crystal clear. The energy of God initiated events that evolved into a universe and a fertile, fruitful planet Earth, according to Genesis. The story is told colloquially in two different ways: in a ritualized setting of seven days and as a folk tale in a garden symbolizing paradise.

The first account gives no hint of the billions of years that preceded the emergence of life on our planet, but gets right down to Earth in a succinct and orderly fashion, exercising the creative prerogative of ritual and myth. The

active engagement of the Divine in the planet's evolutionary process clearly reflects that matter is manifestation of
God's inner spirit and cosmic energy.

The second account imagines how God might have fashioned an earthen creature and transformed it into a living
being by means of the breath of life. Energy breathed into
its nostrils would remain for a lifespan, allowing it to function, numbering its days. Countless examples testify to
how this indwelling Spirit animates and energizes, giving
and sustaining life wherever life is found.

Because the people of biblical times were ordinary folk
like us, there is a fine line separating their experiences
from our own. Their energy is our energy, their inspiration
a lot like ours, which is why phrases, especially from the
psalms, feel like words we might have said at one time or
another.

Where can I go from your spirit, O God? Where can I
flee from your presence? If I skip school, hop a train, fly
across the country or to the other side of the planet, walk
away from my responsibilities, even for a little while, your
spirit, like the hound of heaven, comes galloping after me.
Your energy is everywhere, keeping all in motion. It is solar
energy sending warmth, trade winds circling the globe, the
rippling waters of a mountain stream, the ebb and flow of
oceanic tides, the pull of gravity, the spark that ignites, or
the current that feeds the link to my laptop as these words
come into view, connecting me through electronic means
to anyone anywhere.

Energy rises, energy falls, affecting everything. A broken
spirit is repaired, a troubled spirit is transformed, a lack
of spirit is reawakened, a despondent spirit is renewed.

Energy is ubiquitous. Energy is everywhere. It is the pulse of life. It is another name for spirit.

To be in good spirits is the result of having good energy. Our mood sinks, on the other hand, when energy is depleted or in some way has been blocked. A loss of vitality. A drain of efficiency. We simply can't get it together until energy is restored. Again and again the psalms reveal that the Spirit can revitalize us when we are depressed or so overwhelmed we simply can't go on. Like all those disembodied bones in the vision of Ezekiel, we too will be reenergized when reconnected to our source of empowerment within.

Divine energy flowing through us puts us back together again whenever we fall apart, puts in us a new heart when we become dispirited, reanimates us with a breath of fresh air that gets us moving and motivated to keep on keeping on. Energy generates energy as deep calls to deep, renewing the withered landscape and replenishing planet Earth. This Spirit-charged reality of the Hebrew heritage is fully present in Jesus and through him carries over into the apostolic church.

Jesus, coming out of the waters of his baptism by John, had an experience similar to that of his mother, Mary, before she conceived. He felt a surge of energy and a heightened sense of the Spirit, perceived the heavens opening up and a voice commissioning him for a role that would change his life forever. This child of flesh and Spirit never hesitated, never looked back, and like his courageous mother, accepted the challenge and entered the future, energized by God.

Prior to going public with the mission to which he had been called, Jesus, led by the Spirit, went out into the wilderness on what might be called a vision quest, where he was sorely tempted. For many days and many nights he fasted, prayed, and was confronted by the limits of his humanity, the terrifying taunts of concupiscence, a hunger and thirst for food and drink and the fullness of the Spirit. His indomitable spirit overpowered demonic energy. He emerged from the crisis strengthened and revitalized. Filled with divine energy, Jesus returned to Galilee and, in the synagogue on the Sabbath, spoke the words of Isaiah as he revealed his call from God.

> The Spirit of God is upon me.
> I have been anointed
> to bring good news to the poor,
> to proclaim release to the captives
> and recovery of sight to the blind,
> to liberate those who are oppressed,
> to proclaim the year of favor.
>
> (Luke 4:18–19)

In the few short years before his death, Jesus, filled with the Spirit, healed many as he introduced them to the source of healing within them; preached a liberating word to the impoverished and oppressed; and laid the foundations for a new way of living in solidarity, bound only by the law of love. Crowds followed him everywhere. He raised a lot of energy among the disenfranchised, the curious and the committed, particularly women, and not only locally, but all across the region. This was unacceptable behavior in a nation that was under the control of occupying forces and in a religion where one must adhere to rigidly regulated norms. Stirring up those who are disenchanted and drawing them together are solid threats to the status quo.

Jesus never saw it coming until it was too late. Or perhaps he did, but could not, would not circumvent the Spirit in order to save himself. He told his followers not to worry about what they were going to say if they were apprehended. "Say whatever is given to you at that time," he advised, "for it is not you who speak; it is the Holy Spirit" (Mark 13:11), words to live by in a quantum world where everything is in flux.

Then suddenly, he was gone. Executed. Dead. Buried. And yet, it wasn't over. Some of the women saw him, for their hearts had connected with his in a way that was certain to live on. They let go of the past in order to cling to a living presence. Had they felt his energy? Did they brush against his spirit? Did they sense his aura or catch a glimpse of him through that precious gift of second sight?

It really doesn't matter, because he was truly there, as tangible as intuition to the intuitive, or the lilting tone of a plucked string on a Celtic harp; as real as the massive stone that had sealed the entrance to the tomb but could not halt or inhibit. It didn't matter who believed them or if anyone ever would. They knew what they saw and what they felt, and would not hear otherwise. We have all been there before. We know what it's like when love returns, when we thought it was gone forever. To handle things that cannot be explained, to be able to commune with spirits, to tap into fields of energy, to communicate without words — these were initiation rites into a new Spirit-centered world that Jesus had proclaimed, one that would not be dependent on privilege or priest. The last in line in the old order would be the first to be welcomed in. Anyone could apply.

It all came together in a crowded room where those who had been disciples of Jesus met for mutual support. Sealed within a climate of fear, clutching a tentative wisp of hope, they cringed as the veil between matter and spirit was irrevocably torn apart. Spirit blew open those little locked minds with a force that decimated just about everything they had clung to before. The experience was so explosive they could not keep it to themselves. In a burst of energy, women and men, on fire with the Spirit, poured out into the streets of the city, chaotically proclaiming to everyone God's all-inclusive love.

That spirit carried over into the apostolic church. Divisions of class and gender dissolved. Enthusiastic gatherings around a meal were charged with precious memories that would remain sacrosanct and with a strong sense of the living spirit of Jesus present there among them. Over in Corinth, in Gentile territory, the community brought together by Paul claimed extraordinary gifts of the Spirit with Pentecostal energy but without a historical basis for understanding the movement to which they belonged. Perhaps it was fear that such enthusiastic extremes might threaten unity that resulted in a tempering of spirit, a regulation of expression, and a redirection of energy into predetermined rites. By the time early eyewitnesses had died, energetic spontaneity was only intermittent at best and, in time, faded away.

The divine all-encompassing Spirit of God is dynamic energy, chaotic energy creating and re-creating, continually giving impetus to that which is beyond anything we can ever hope to express. Spirit calls out to spirit. A profusion of energy during his life and an energized spirit after his death linked Jesus to everyone who had kept faith with him. That living spirit continues to connect us in spirit to Jesus today.

Death-into-life reality, from which all that is emerges and to which all will return, is the matrix of our being and the wellspring of our becoming. The presence and the power of Spirit-charged energy will not be constrained by rationality, no matter how hard institutions try to limit it by laws. That which is elusive and ephemeral and eternal cannot be contained, cannot be controlled. God's free-flowing spirit liberates and will not be bound. Spirit is at the heart of all that is, was, and will be, and is in some way one with our own being and becoming.

Spirit is the channel of divine energy and that Spirit is within us. There is one spirit only. The Spirit of Jesus, your spirit and mine, are emanations of the Divine. Spirit of God is Energy in everything, everyone, everywhere.

Quanta

It is a risk to take a term identified with something as specific as a new scientific theory and use it somewhere else, but I want to do it anyway, because it is key to developing a quantum-based spirituality. There is precedent in Christian tradition for this kind of approach. In the developmental stages of the apostolic church, newly emerging communities appropriated words, concepts, practices, and even psalms and hymns that already had a history in vastly different settings and reinterpreted them. Original meanings changed through use. Eventually, what had once been borrowed was seen as integral to that which had given birth to something new.

Quanta: chunk of energy that is invisible to the eye, a unit of energy that is revealed through its visible effects. Quanta, as a metaphor, is ideally suited for bridging the gap between science and spirituality. While maintaining its integrity in the area where it originated, it brings to the other side of the spectrum a rich bundle of associations that will in time help to forge an alliance between the two. Quanta is now that chunk of energy that personifies you and me. In earlier times the metaphor was temple — a sanctuary, a vessel, a container for the Spirit of God, the energy of God. That which holds the Divine is holy. We are filled with divine energy. The human body, our body, is a holy place.

The energies of the universe, abiding and expanding, energy fields, particle and wave, flow in and out of every one of us in forms that render us human. Eight energy systems cooperate within us, shaping us and sustaining us from birth to final breath. Our private moods, our public face, how we feel, how we behave reflect our internal energy flow far more than we realize.

When energy is blocked, siphoned off, or completely drained, the visible effects are far too often attributed to other causes, when we may just lack the physical and psychic energy to go on. When energy is high and flowing freely, we have verve, style, soul, élan, charisma that draws people to us, or enthusiasm that lets others know we are at the top of our game.

Ancients called this *mana*,[23] a supernatural force with magical powers. We simply say, this is who we are. This very best aspect of our persona is our most valuable asset and the source of our personal power.

Let us take a quick look at three of the eight forms of energy that are vital to our existence — our meridians, chakras, and aura.

Meridians are pathways that move energy into us and out of us and throughout our entire body, connecting hundreds of acupuncture points of energy on our skin. Meridians allow energy to flow through all our organs and physiological systems. They adjust our metabolism and revitalize us, so that we are able to get up each morning and continue on through the day. Like the rhythmic rush of the air we breathe and the coursing of blood through arteries and veins, the flow of energy within us is critical to life. When balanced and aligned to Earth's meridians, our energy pathways pulsate with cosmic energy.

Chakras are energy centers situated at seven sites within us, from the base of our spine to the top of our head and at five points in between. Each of the seven chakras channels energy through those parts of our body within its field of influence, encoding memories at a cellular level by imprinting emotional traumas and significant experiences we would otherwise forget.

At the base of the spine is the root chakra, the life force within us essential to our survival. Its foundational energy grounds us, linking us to the primal, generative energies of Earth. It connects us to other people and to other people's passion and gives impetus to the feeling that all of us are one. Here is the source of our basic drives and our instinctive reactions. Here is where we sink our roots and forge an identity.

The second, or womb, chakra safeguards creativity and imagination and nurtures the free spirit of the child before it has been molded into a competitor or a survivor. There is an aspect of innocence associated with this energy, and of hospitality. People feel at home with one who is energized by this chakra. Here we trust intuition as our primary guide.

The third, or solar plexus, chakra is the source of our personal power. It asserts itself definitively and in terms of our achievements. A strong sense of identity shaped by the pressure of expectations and the ups and downs of maturing indicates that logic and individuality are predominant here.

The fourth, which is the heart chakra, is source of our energies of compassion and love. It connects us to others, heart to heart, deeply and intensely. While it is possible to love too much and to feel too much of another's pain, it is essential to immerse ourselves in the energy of this chakra, for it is here that we love unconditionally and grow in loving all.

The fifth, or throat, chakra is the center of our self-expression. Energies of all the other chakras pass through here as through a hub where vital information is rearranged, synthesized, and integrated into the core of who we are, or who we say we are, thereby defining the unique way we present ourselves to the world.

The sixth, which is the pituitary, also called the third eye chakra, is where our sense of separateness from all else is transcended, where we hone our ability to perceive that which the eye cannot see and to commune with worlds beyond us. Here is where we are at ease with mystery and meaning, where symbols and abstractions do not have to be explained.

The seventh, or crown, chakra, located on the very top of our head, opens us up to the cosmos and to gifts from the Spirit that flow like a river of love and light into us and through us. Here, what we receive in abundance moves down to our roots and throughout our entire body before being sent out into the universe as a blessing to all.

A third form of energy in us is what is known as an aura. Our aura is an energy zone surrounding us like a protective shield. It consists of our own energy emanating from our body and it interacts with those energies we encounter all around us, drawing beneficial energy in and dispersing energies we send out. It changes in size, shape, and color according to our mood and our physical condition, expanding to fill the space we are in when we are feeling expansive, and closing in, even collapsing, whenever we shut down.

Our meridians, chakras, and aura are part of a complex network of energy keeping us in existence. This massive flow of energy that sustains humanity and delineates every one of us as distinct individuals is part of a larger energy grid that constitutes the cosmos. Energy flows back and forth from here to there and from there to here, spiraling within us, around us, beyond us in ways we have yet to imagine and still do not understand. We are influenced by this energy. At the same time our own energy has influence as well. We see the effects of this daily and are only beginning to explore the possibilities of its potential.

While experimenting with the formation of water crystals, Japanese scientist Masaru Emoto discovered that, prior to the emergence of crystals, the water seemed to be aware of positive and negative stimuli and would respond accordingly an astonishing number of times. The experiment began with music and then moved on to words, which were written on pieces of paper. A word was attached to each container so that it faced the water. When shown a word such as "hate," the crystals that emerged were ugly or deformed, while words such as "love" and "thank you" gave rise to crystals that were absolutely beautiful. He repeated the experiment numerous times with similar results. Water seemed to react by forming crystals appropriate to stimuli. It was as if the water knew what was being said to it, orally or in writing, and adjusted its response.[24]

Dr. Emoto attributes this synchronicity to frequencies, or vibrations, in other words, energy. Everything vibrates to a frequency. When a single frequency sound wave forms between two entities, there is harmonic resonance. Musicians understand this in relationship to sound. Quantum theorists have been working with frequencies for over a century. The rest of us are only beginning to experience what this implies.

Energy is in everything, in matter and in motion. All matter is in motion. Motion is kinetic energy. Matter is energy of being. This is the stuff we are made of. Matter and motion. Particle and wave. Forms of energy. Appearing and disappearing. Vibrating. Undulating. Interacting. Interchanging. Weaving, waving, darting, dancing. The quantumstuff of the universe is pure energy, and it is everywhere.

Energy is the matrix for a quantum-based spirituality. Quantum spirituality — energy spirituality — will find

its root metaphors in that which evokes and intercon-
nects the energies of the universe and the fields of energy
on planet Earth, linking all to divine energy, its primordial source. In quanta, chunks of energy, and interlocking
fields of energy, are seeds for planetary transformation and
for bringing to fulfillment that ethereal promise of peace.

The results of the study on water and words are provoca-
tive. If words can influence water, imagine their impact
on people. Sticks and stones do break bones, but words
can be more destructive, wounding in ways that may
never heal, carrying over to the next generation when left
unreconciled.

On the other hand words can also make amends for a
past injustice, forge alliances for peace, mend a ruptured
relationship, heal a hurt, seal a promise, assure the love
we feel for one another is for real. Energy, whether in water
or words or in people who are made up of water and words,
transmits the renewing effects of good or the devastation
of evil. Imagine the possibilities of sending all around the
world a word of love, a word of compassion, words of
healing and hope and peace by sending positive energy
outward, sending it again, and still again, until more and
more people all over the world are on a single frequency
and vibrating with love.

Energy is a conduit for the Divine in and around
us. Imagine quanta, chunks of energy, connecting and
coalescing, whirling, twirling toward the tipping point,
overflowing with love.

Chapter 6

Modes of
a Quantum Spirit

Modes
are ways and means
of Being,
ways and means
of Spirit being
present
active
effective
in
our universe
our many worlds
our individual lives.
In and through
the quantum modes of
chaos
consciousness
connection
Spirit infiltrates spirit
to reach our chaotic
not fully conscious
disconnected selves,
to motivate and integrate,
to instigate and inspire.

In this manner
matter
behaves like waves of energy
reverberating, resonating, replicating
grace.

Chaos

I kept saying to myself, just do it. Stop stalling and write that book. But I couldn't sit down to write about chaos, because life was so chaotic.

Everything around me, even within me, seemed to be spinning out of control, and I could do nothing to stop it. "I need time to write my book," I shouted to no one in particular one really wild winter day, and to my absolute amazement, a response ricocheted back to me from the belly of the beast. "What do you think you've been doing? You have been *living* your book. It is already there within you."

Isn't it ironic? I create and teach from experience, talk endlessly about how wisdom is revealed on every page of the book of life, yet I failed to get the message that was so clearly meant for me. It wasn't time that I needed. I probably could have found the time if I had not missed the point. I wanted an end to chaos before sitting down to write about it. I wanted things to be under control before reflecting on relinquishing control. Now that's paradox. When I finally saw the light, the floodgates opened and I was immersed in paradoxology.

Chaos is integral to life. This is a quantum discovery. Yet our instinctive reaction is to eliminate chaos and return to the way things ought to be. Most of us can tolerate a bit of chaos here and there, but only now and then. When will we ever learn it is the norm and not the exception? Chaos is an organizing principle of our quantum universe. For this reason chaos theory is essential to quantum physics.

Chaos has ancient literary and metaphysical roots. In Greek mythology, Chaos is the gaping void, the bottomless, limitless chasm. It is nothingness before the beginning of time. It is prelude to existence. Creation myths around the world speak of a primordial Chaos from which all else emerged.

Gaia came out of Chaos in the form of planet Earth. Throughout the ancient Near East, Chaos was the formless void, the vast expanse of emptiness, a dark cosmic womb. A Mesopotamian myth says the world was fashioned out of the dismembered body of Tiamat, the personification of Chaos.

A creation account in the Bible states that the genesis of all that is originated in an interaction between the spirit of the living God and the vast and formless void. In the beginning, there was nothing. In the beginning, there was chaos. Life springs from chaos, is formed, and then transformed.

Chaos is life as it is, not as we would like it to be, or as most spiritual directives suggest, we discipline ourselves to be. Life itself is chaos as it tests and tempers all that transpires, spoiling our good intentions, making a mess of things. At the same time life delineates the contours of our spirituality, not because of a smooth sailing through uneventful circumstances, but because it offers opportunities to confront chaotic disruptions and learn how to take them in stride as we grow spiritually.

If chaos is reflective of who we are and represents where we have come from, how is it that we know so little about what to do with it? We declare that something is out of control when we really mean out of our control. We are so accustomed to taking charge that even self-control means the imposition of order. We demand predictability. We thrive on set routines. We plan ahead, show up prepared, have a time and place for everything only to come undone when something unexpected happens. Quantum reality cannot be forced into frameworks we impose. We need to trust that the inherent capacity for order that exists in nature and within each one of us will eventually take its course. Sometimes the universe intervenes simply to remind us that we are part of something larger than our rigidly ordered selves. As sojourners here on planet Earth, we are beneficiaries of a nurturing largesse, an ancient hospitality that is flexible and adaptive and, consequently, very wise. A particular outcome or series of events may not be what we intended, but for reasons we may never know, what happens was meant to be.

Chaos, like the air we breathe, is an existential element of what we do and who we are. It is matrix for the roles we play within the universe story, evoking improvisational twists in our ever-evolving lives. We have been conditioned to seek equilibrium and eliminate disorder. Chaos tips the balance toward the things we would avoid. Internalized attitudes tell us that chaos is our enemy, reiterating a past paradigm that can no longer support us in the world in which we live.

In a quantum universe, we have to make friends with chaos. As the world becomes more and more complex, and unpredictable, as global interactions intensify and technology entices us to take on more than we can manage, we will meet chaos at every turn. We must learn to live with it, because, in the words of Walter Cronkite, "That's the way it is." And that's the way it is going to be well into the foreseeable future.

While I was immersed in a new paradigm, part of me was still stuck in the old, and I did not know it. Although imagination and new ideas were pulling me away from the old ways with which I had once been satisfied, deep-rooted formalities continued to hold me fast. It was only in and through chaos that I was able to find the path that led to an inner freedom.

According to chaos theory, complex natural systems will break their own self-governing rules when infinitesimal changes occur within, giving rise to unexpected and unpredictable outcomes. All living organisms have this innate capacity to order and transform themselves. What may seem completely chaotic to us is nature's way of reorganizing and effecting systemic change. Chaos moves us forward, for it is hard to cling to our set ways when confronted by forces that turn our expectations upside down. Such change is often dramatic, but it can also be quite subtle. The smallest change in a quantum matrix can have huge repercussions. A butterfly flapping its wings in Brazil can trigger tornadoes in Texas. This is the well-known "butterfly effect" promulgated by chaos theory. Small changes lead to big effects, and when sufficient change has occurred, an entity is transformed.[25]

Paradigmatic shifts take time to finally fall into place. We cannot hurry macro movement, no matter how many micro changes are happening all at once. We may know we are in a quantum world, but we have absolutely no idea of what that really means. It is hard to be in transition. Who among us feels at home in the throes of paradox? We are still unaware of how strongly we cling to assumptions and behaviors that prevent our seriously entering into a quantum frame of mind. The challenge for quantum spirituality will be to facilitate a new way of thinking and a more compassionate way of relating to those within our immediate world and the multitudes beyond it.

One can only imagine the chaos surrounding the death of Jesus and the turbulent time of transition for his followers and friends. Here was one whose vision held promise for the future, until all that he stood for drifted away like dry leaves in the wind. The hopes of the disenfranchised, a cause that gave the poor something tangible to cling to, disappeared when he died. Then in one chaotic moment, devastation was reversed. Pentecost erupted with the realization his spirit would live on.

All of us are caught up in complex situations. We have multiple responsibilities and minimal disposable time. Yet this is when God expects us to live spiritually responsible lives. Not when things get better. Not when the frenzy tapers off or ceases altogether. Not when we retire. Now. In the midst of whatever is happening, we are to acknowledge God's paradoxical presence and lift up our hearts in praise.

Because we are accustomed to seeking spiritual sustenance in a setting of serenity, we are clueless to signs of the Spirit that are right in front of us whenever chaos erupts. As long as we confine the Spirit to those old familiar places earmarked by tradition, we will not comprehend the transformative truth that chaos is God's spirit in Pentecostal mode.

Spirituality in a quantum universe is not a retreat from chaos but reconciliation with it. When we enter the void at the core of chaos and become one with it, we merge with that creative vitality in and through which something new is always given life. More often than not what appears to be an irritating interruption in our day-to-day routine morphs into a main event, or merges with our mission, or becomes the beginning of something we have been patiently awaiting, a turn of events that affects us deeply and may even substantially change us.

Fidelity to the Spirit is the sine qua non for all who desire to be catalysts of compassion and sustaining grace. Whenever we say yes to the Spirit, even when we are inclined to say no, converging energies coalesce to energize and bless. God's spirit is in the chaos, in the turbulent wind, the fire and flame, the cacophony and confusion. Spirit's voice vibrates at its very core. God's spirit is chaos. The void and the vortex are one and the same. Chaos and Spirit are one.

Consciousness

Again and again the surging sea comes rolling in and onto the sand, tossing a spray of crystal confetti into the rays of the sun. What does the sea know of its role in a vast and varied universe? I know a deep and satisfying peace as I watch its rhythmic movements, am aware of how revitalized I feel when I'm wading in its waters, searching for shells and that part of myself that disintegrates in concrete canyons.

The sea is unaware of me and of its own significance, and yet it is part of a primordial energy permeating all. The universe is imbued with consciousness of one kind or another. Our planet in particular is a living, breathing entity pulsating with life, which means we need to reconsider how we relate to life here on Earth in all of its manifestations.

Consciousness, as we understand it, is characteristic of sentient beings. Simply put, to be conscious is to be aware, and to be human is to have the capacity to reflect upon that awareness. You and I are made of the very same molecular matter as stars, stones, and surging seas, flowering fields and canopied forests, yet these stunning displays of nature are impervious to their capacity to generate wonder and awe in us. Or so we have believed.

We share genetic traits with animals and insects, claim a common ancestry that emerged from the water, slithered, scurried, climbed, clawed, ran like the wind over solid ground, even flew up and into the skies. Yet we are the ones through whom the universe reflects upon itself, because we are self-reflective. We are the only ones with this innate capacity. Or so we have believed.

What is reflective consciousness? Are we alone in this? Or is it possible that animals, and even the birds and the bees, know more than they can tell?

Thank you, I say to the mockingbird, when I wake to its intoxicating song in the middle of the night. Its lilting motifs echo the music of a planetary soul, introducing melodies of amazing intricacy. Does the mockingbird know it mimics the songs other birds sing throughout the day? Is it aware it arranges them into a choral symphony? And is this purposeful? A quantum universe gives rise to questions such as these.

Dogs. Cats. Horses. Pigs. Anyone who has a pet has stories they can tell. The communal activities of bees and ants, the behavior of dolphins and animals in the wild seem akin to a higher consciousness similar to our own. "You go, girls!" I shouted, when I read that three female elephants in the Bronx Zoo had looked at themselves in a mirror and discovered they could inspect those parts of their body they were unable to see before.[26] I wonder what they were thinking. "Better ease up on the bananas." "My, look at those curves." "I need some Oil of Olay."

From the dawn of civilization, indigenous peoples have honored a primal level of consciousness shared with stones, the wind, the trees, the land, and all God's creatures, great and small. Biologist Lyall Watson has this to say.

> There is an exchange of information at a very basic level between all living things...which allows even radically different organisms, as different as a man and a bush, to borrow each other's ideas.[27]

As we move deeper into a quantum understanding of our expanding universe, perhaps many more of us will one day feel the same. Humanity has situated itself at the pinnacle of creation. Now may be the time to reassess this claim.

We share consciousness on some level with all life on our planet, and in a variety of ways, we hone the gift we were given. Through mindfulness and attentiveness and awareness and perception, we make a conscious effort to focus, and to be fully present, and to broaden our perspective. The conscientiousness of our consciousness hinges on perception. It has to do with perspective. It depends on what we see.

The blind Bartimaeus begged Jesus for one thing only. He cried out: "I want to see" (Mark 10:46–52). We can be certain Bartimaeus was blessed with more than physical sight, for seeing, according to Jesus, is about more than meets the eye. There is sight and then there is insight. Seeing happens when something clicks, when someone sees the light. "I get it!" "Yes!" "Aha!" "Eureka!" "I was blind, but now I see."

The male disciples who followed Jesus just didn't get it. They did not see what he could see, which is why they could not comprehend the full extent of his vision. They remained entrenched in their limitations, while Jesus saw beyond them. Caught up in the politics of power, they were lost when he was apprehended. It was different with the women, who also accompanied him and were among his closest friends. They sensed something deeper and continued to feel his living presence after he was gone. "I have seen him" (John 20:18), cried Mary Magdalene to the astonished disciples. Other women also saw him, but those who were their leaders, we are told, did not believe them. Seeing is believing. That's the way it usually is. Put all your cards on the table. Show me what you've got. "Unless I see the mark of the nails, I will not believe," said Thomas (John 20:25). Jesus appeared, showed him the wounds, and doubting Thomas was a believer.

In the physical world, the extent to which we can see is limited. However, through the eyes of faith, we can see forever. For the dubious and the distrustful, seeing is believing, but for those imbued with a consciousness envisioned by Jesus, believing is seeing. The kind of belief we are talking about is not a rational function but a depth experience that penetrates to the bone. Whoever is perceptive knows a world of magic and mystics, of impossible dreams and improbable deeds, of poets and prophets and saints, where the cognitive trusts intuition, where reason reverences feeling, where imagination is paramount. Insight reveals what the eye cannot see. Sensitivity helps the heart comprehend. This realm of Spirit-filled consciousness that Jesus proclaimed through his life and his death is the divine milieu. It is already present, among us and within us, and it is possible to discern it if we only had eyes to see.

Perception is the lens through which we see the world around us, delineating good from evil, the alien from our neighbor, the enemy from our friend. If our focus is distorted, if the aperture is too narrow, if our viewpoint is predetermined, we will see only what we want to see and be none the wiser for it. The sufferings of humanity will continue to spiral out of control, wars will go on unabated, and planet Earth will fall into the void, one ice floe at a time.

In a world that is now more accessible than ever but much less understood, we need to be careful that our perceptions of other cultures and other religions are not misconstrued. We dare not call someone an enemy who is at heart a friend. A quantum universe has myriad paths and endless variations. It all makes sense when we look at it through the loving eyes of Divinity. Then we can see, as God sees, that an undivided consciousness is the basis for being one. This divine consciousness continues to elude our understanding, even as it gathers us in and evokes our assent.

That I might hold to you the more closely, I would that my consciousness were as wide as the skies and the earth and the peoples of the earth; as deep as the past, the desert, the ocean; as tenuous as the atoms of matter or the thoughts of the human heart.[28]

What is this strange phenomenon that is said to permeate all? Teilhard de Chardin knew, albeit intuitively.
Even so, he surely had questions similar to our own. Is
there a universal Mind? a cosmic Wisdom? a conscious
Knowing? We can only describe consciousness. We cannot
really define it. What it is lies well beyond our ability to
comprehend it.

Consciousness may be embodied, but it lacks concrete
physicality. It is the essence of being, like the smell of
perfume, the warmth of the sun, the sound of a song, the
raw experience of life itself, of laughter, loss, anxiety, relief,
the feeling of forgiveness, the sense of exultation in the
aftermath of grace, the solid yet illusive sense of loving
and being loved.

Consciousness is at the core of an emerging spirituality
in this quantum universe, for consciousness, like energy,
is mysteriously pervasive. We speak of divine consciousness, yet all consciousness is divine. It is a mode of divinity
whereby Spirit is present in and to and through each and
every one of us and every aspect of creation.

This consciousness that is shared by all holds a wellspring of hope for our present age and unlimited possibilities for that which is to come. There is a world beyond
this world poised to emerge here and now to fulfill our
desire for a paradise lost and not for a paradise delayed
until everything comes to an end. If enough of us are
convinced that this can happen, then it will, for infinite
consciousness transcends our finite limitations.

A convergence of global consciousness can give rise to
a groundswell of whatever on Earth is needed for the
dawning of that day. This is the sense in which consciousness creates reality. Through hindsight, foresight,

insight, from outside in and inside out, through another's needs and one another's pain, through the prism of all the world's cultural and spiritual perspectives, we reach into the future and evoke its transforming synergy on behalf of our present time. The consciousness of all that ever was and all that is unfolding has always been, will always be, incomprehensibly one.

Connection

Right up there with our longing to belong and our yearning to be loved is our need to be connected. It is the driving force behind our obsession with text messaging, cell phone conversations, and Internet exchanges.

These modes of communication, once considered a luxury, are fast becoming necessities of contemporary life. Yet beneath the surface, is it really that different from what we did in the past? The means and methods may have changed with advances in technology and an increase in mobility, yet the inner urge to keep in touch and to keep intact the ties that bind is the same as it always was. Our passion for hooking up is more than a generational hang-up. It is a genetic predisposition born of our interconnectedness within the web of life. The impetus to connect is humanity's reenactment of the ways of the universe.

The fetus in the womb depends upon a life-sustaining connection for growth and development. Its umbilical cord may be cut when the baby moves out into the wider world, but the invisible link between mother and child can never be fully severed. Even if the relationship falters or fails to come to fruition, a trace of that natal bond remains imprinted deep within. Kids may appear to outgrow a predilection for family connections in their rush to relate to their peers, but the inclination resurfaces when they too have children, and eventually it solidifies as their children and their grandchildren have children of their own.

While it may not always seem that way, family ties are strengthened whenever we interact. Birthdays. Weddings. Funerals. Taking our place at the table for the traditional Thanksgiving meal. Coming home for Christmas. Family events reconnect us, all the way down to our roots, creating sacramental moments to mark the relentless passage of time as we celebrate our lives. Even when there is tension, or dissent, or a history of alienation, even when there are family members who remain unreconciled, efforts to reach out and welcome them in leave a microcosmic mark invisibly, unfailingly. These seeds sown by the Spirit are there to be harvested at some future time.

We live in a quantum universe where connections are never static. They vibrate with potential, for the energy fields that surround us and the energies within us are forever poised to surprise us when we are least prepared. We are only a heartbeat away from a total turnaround of a troubling situation. If we live in anticipation of forgiving and being forgiven, opportunities to do just that will suddenly abound. We will never know ahead of time the moment for a miracle. We just need to be ready with an open mind and an open heart should that moment come to pass. Miracles do happen, as when an age-old grudge is lifted or a prodigal child comes home.

Our genealogical energy stream is unique and irreplaceable, a thread that has been interwoven into the cosmic web. It extends back through our ancestors, century after century, to and through the ancients, the hominids, our primate past, all the way back to the genesis of that first microbial blip of life, connecting us through the ages to everything that is.

> When we try to pick out anything by itself, we find it hitched to everything else in the universe.[29]

Invisible waves of energy link canyon and cave, tundra and town, the full sweep of genus and species, extant and extinct. The seas, the trees, the birds and the bees, our diverse nationalities are in some way connected. All of us are connected. "Six degrees of separation."[30] It takes six steps, no more, they say, and maybe even less, to establish a connection between any two people through existing linkages. Then why is it so hard for us to live collaboratively? Thomas Aquinas, thirteenth-century scholastic, one of the most influential theologians within Roman Catholic tradition, wrote:

> How is it they live for eons in such harmony —
> the billions of stars —
> when most men can barely go a minute
> without declaring war in their mind
> against someone they know.
> There are wars where no one marches with a flag,
> though that does not keep casualties from mounting.
> Our hearts irrigate this earth.
> We are fields before each other.
> How can we live in harmony?
> First we need to know
> we are all madly in love
> with the same God.[31]

It is simply not enough to say that we are all connected. We need to honor that connection by appreciating
the richness of each unique genealogical thread woven
into our worldwide web. We also need to realize that we
who say there is a God are all in love with the same
God. Through multiple manifestations, revelations, incarnations, the spirit of our living God is reaching out to us,
connecting us to one another and through the Spirit to all
creation within the divine milieu.

The intergalactic harmony of which Aquinas so elo-
quently spoke has another tempestuous side that can also
be found in us. Black holes devour, gas clouds destroy, and
the smaller of two cosmic entities is strangled and stripped
when galaxies clash. This violent streak and a tendency to
erupt are also our heritage. We who have evolved to where
intention can tame this destructiveness have a responsibility not to disrupt the universe with our recklessness and
our rage.

On the cusp of the twenty-first century, we caught a
glimpse of apocalyptic peace as the dawn of a new millennium jubilantly encircled the planet, heralding shalom.
On the stroke of midnight, nation after nation reveled in
the radiance of a global harmonic convergence. Many of
us tried to imagine what it might be like if the cultural interconnectedness of Earth's huddled masses would still be
there when night disappeared and we woke to the morning light. Symbols are meant to uplift us and to remind us
that what has happened once can also happen again. As
symbol, that memorable millennial moment is precious
and profound.

Our twenty-first century world is one in which good and
evil, life and death, those who have enough and more than

enough and those who are deprived live in close proximity, no matter how far apart. We are all bound together within a divine milieu. How we live as individuals and what we do as a society are bound to affect us all. As difficult as it is for some to admit, the God we praise in traditions that differ radically from each other is not a God of division but of diversity. Ancient sages understood the power within this claim, knew without reservation that there is one universal Spirit integrating all.

It may be said that we are the product of our lifelong connections, a hub of connectivity in the network that is our life. We mediate and facilitate and communicate on many levels. We are conduits of energy for building up and tearing down and making all things new. Forming bonds and building bridges are our gifts to the universe. Links that lead to destructive deeds are the wounds we leave behind.

Since we are all connected, let us make the most of it by moving beyond the banal and searching for opportunities to join forces and pool resources for the greater good. Spirit linked to spirit can transcend our limitations, moving with the speed of light to liberate and bless.

Chapter 7

Manifestations of a Quantum Spirit

Coincidence
Creation
Celebration
manifestations
of the Spirit
manifestations
of our spirit
impression of Divinity
expression of Eternity
visible
incarnate
animate
among us and within us.
Self-revealing, Self-disclosing
Spirit of God
to our spirit
through our spirit
reveals mere matter
is not merely matter.
We are
particularly
and

spectacularly
particles of divinity
Divine particularity
in bits and bytes and electrolytes:
Epiphany
Divinity
made manifestly real.

Coincidence

Coincidence is commonplace in a quantum universe peppered with paradox. Far too many people are unaware of this. I'd like to tell some stories to illustrate how coincidence is trademark of the Spirit in our daily lives.

A conference I did not want to attend, because I had too much to do, set in motion a series of events that would rearrange my life. I found myself in Cleveland, where I met Ludmila Javorová, a Roman Catholic priest, who, in 1970, had been secretly ordained behind the Iron Curtain in Czechoslovakia's underground Church.

Ludmila had been invited to visit the United States, and in the process of breaking her silence, to consider writing a book. I was captivated by her story, but when the weekend was over, I went on with the rest of my life. The following week I took the train from Connecticut to Philadelphia. We hadn't gone very far when I heard a familiar voice in a language I could not understand reverberating across the aisle. "Ludmila!" I shouted, absolutely amazed at seeing her again. She and her Czech companions were on their way to Washington, D.C., before returning home. It was a quantum moment. We continued on together until we reached New York, where they decided to get off and see the city, since they were already there.

Later that week I awoke with a start in the middle of the night. "I am going to write the book that they had talked about in Cleveland," I said. This was news to me, for it was not on my agenda. In the morning I called my publisher. He said they had just decided to publish Ludmila's story. He had been told to give me a call and ask me to write the book.

Coincidence? Definitely. And that was just the beginning. The collaboration between Ludmila and me was filled with coincidence, paradoxical occurrences, unequivocal manifestations of a quantum Spirit.

Ludmila and I share a deep awareness of the Spirit in our lives. In the aftermath of Vatican II, we struggled to discern the signs of the times in our respective settings on opposite sides of the ocean, one in a context of freedom, the other in an environment of hostility and fear. My experience in the 1960s consisted of an experimental Mass in what was called an underground church in the Archdiocese of Philadelphia. Our only concern had to do with when they might come and close us down. The real underground church, an invisible entity whose many members were sworn to secrecy, was in Czechoslovakia. Because religious affiliation was restricted to state-approved institutions, participation was against the law. The threat of imprisonment, even death, followed Ludmila daily for more than twenty years.

Our worlds could not have been more different, yet beneath the surface a commitment to be open to the Spirit and faithful to God's unpredictable ways was very much the same. It was a thread of continuity, this unshakeable substratum of hope, linking us to each other and to all who claim to be church when authorities think otherwise. Although Ludmila spoke no English and I did not know a word of Czech, I had no doubt, and neither did she, that Spirit who had brought the two of us together would help us to accomplish what we had set out to do. "If you had not come to me," she once said, "I would have had to find you." Both of us knew instinctively that what she said was true.

After several transatlantic trips to interview Ludmila, I returned to the Czech Republic in order to write the book. As I was recording the fatal illness and death of Ludmila's brother, Frantisek, I began to cry. An enormous sorrow engulfed me. "Why am I crying?" I asked myself. "I never even knew him." A day or so later the telephone rang. "Your mother is dying. Don't delay. Come home as soon as you can."

I began yet another journey into the unknown. Because the weekend had already started, my translators were unavailable. Airline offices were closed. "You who are with me as who you will be, be with me as who I need you to be," was the mantra I prayed, over and over, trusting that Spirit who had led me here would surely lead me home.

My plan was to keep moving westward until I reached the Unites States. The bus to Vienna, however, called for Austrian currency, which I did not have. A stranger, who was fluent in English, offered to assist me with my bus fare and my bags. We boarded the bus together. I discovered that my angel guide was a Muslim Kurd in exile, active in the underground liberation movement in Iraq. He had a daughter whose name was Miriam. He spoke passionately of peace and love, echoing what I had been saying for years. "We are all one," he insisted. "God loves every-one." In Vienna he carried my unwieldy luggage, helped me find the bus for the international airport, and waited until I was safely settled before vanishing into the night as mysteriously as he had come.

The flight to London was booked solid. So was the flight to New York. I was told it would be impossible to leave within the next two days. "Be with me, Holy Spirit," I prayed. I told the attendant my mom was dying. She excused herself, and when she returned, she had boarding passes in her hand. Although the flight itself is a blur, I vividly recall landing in New York amid torrential rains and tumultuous winds that chased us to the ground. Ours was the last flight to land that evening. The bus from JFK to Hartford wove in and out of an electrical storm of singular ferocity. I arrived home just before midnight. On Sunday. Pentecost!

My mother was not fully conscious, although she acknowledged me with her eyes. I was told I had already been there before I had arrived. My mom had thought I was physically present when she saw me standing beside her bed, but I had been there in spirit. "What are you doing here?" she had asked. "You should be over there writing your book." It was like when she had come to me in a dream a few weeks earlier. We both knew the end was approaching, that her cancer had returned, but she said she would wait until after my trip before coming to live with me. When I fell asleep that night, I heard her call my name, like a primal scream hurled out of an abyss. I sat up in bed and said aloud, "I'm coming, Mom. Tomorrow!" I awoke to a phone call from her. She cried out my name exactly as I had heard it in my dream and asked me to come and get her because she needed to be with me.

Mom died on the Octave of Pentecost. Her first act from the other side may have been to arrange her funeral to be meaningful for me. The pastor at her parish church, a former Episcopalian, was a married priest. His pastoral associate was a woman. We sang some of my songs at the liturgy, sang about blessing and a mothering God. I presided at her graveside service, altering images and words from the traditional prayer book for a more inclusive celebration.

While we were in the neighborhood, I went to our former parish church, where my mom's faith had been nurtured and where I had prayed as a child. All the old statues were still keeping vigil behind their votive lamps. In one time-less moment this radical feminist knelt before the statue of our Blessed Mother. I lit a candle for my mom, Irene, and felt the cosmic connection between my world here and her world there somewhere over the rainbow. The mother of Jesus, my mother, and I are so deeply intertwined in spirit I can feel the womb-love pulsating, linking us as one. We are present to each other in an eternal now; for in God's time, quantum time, past and present are one.

In the weeks that followed I sat with my laptop out under the trees and went back to writing my book. Chipmunks have long been signs to me of connection to the spirit world. For years there have been two or three in residence behind my house. Within days after my mother's funeral, suddenly, there were five. One of them came right up to me and ate seeds out of my hand.

Life is full of those moments when the spirit of the living God tries to get through to us. Once in a while the attempt to establish contact is crystal clear. Here is another example.

God knows I have missed making music. There has seldom been time or space to sing or be brazenly intuitive in theological education. I had made a new year's resolution to do something about it and was praying for direction when I received another one of those phone calls. My brother Bob had died.

A retired university professor in the field of physics, he was conservative, and definitive, so we avoided talking about certain things, like politics and religion, and, yes, quantum physics. Although he and I were as different as two people can be, he was genuinely supportive of me and he was beginning to mellow. He liked the earlier songs I had written and recorded and he had sent some of my books as gifts to each of his six children. One day, shortly before he died, he telephoned and said to me, "You are a very good writer," words I will always cherish. Then he added, "However, I don't always agree with you," which wasn't a surprise.

Bob's home was in southern Pennsylvania. His children couldn't wait to show me the play list on his computer. Among his top twenty-five favorites were eighteen of my songs. On the night table beside his bed was my most recent book and it had a telltale bookmark. All my other books were stacked in a pile on the dining room table and appeared to have been used. A lot. All this, and I never knew it.

The funeral liturgy was moving. Each of his six children spoke, from the eldest to the youngest. So did two Knights of Columbus, a fraternal organization in which Bob held a very high rank. I too stepped to the podium. "I am Bob's left-wing, off-the-wall, radical feminist sister," I began, in an attempt at full disclosure. And that was how I discovered he had many liberal friends, that he had done many good works on behalf of those in need, that there was another side to him that he had never revealed to me, a side that was a lot like me.

Driving through the rolling hills on the long ride back to Hartford, I felt my brother's presence, chatted with him and sang gospel songs along with the radio. I reminded the Spirit of my longing to sing a new song of my own. Dark clouds hovered all the way home, but always on the sidelines. I passed rainbow after rainbow until the seventh and final one. It straddled the road with vibrant arches like a gateway into the Eternal, and I went sailing through. There had to be a message in all that I was experiencing and in all that I was feeling, and I knew that at the appropriate time, it would be revealed to me.

Several days after I returned, as I sat in my women's leadership circle, I heard the deep and mesmerizing sound of a large Celtic harp. Later, when I plucked its strings, the tones vibrated within me, making of me the song. "Where did this come from?" I asked Marisa, to whom the harp belonged. It had been handmade for her by a craftsman named Al Winters (imagine!), who lived in Pennsylvania in the vicinity where I had just come from, on the other side of those rainbows, not far from by brother's home. Gotcha! Spirit whispered, as it all fell into place.

The harp was the gateway to the song my soul longed to be singing, the treasure at the end of those rainbows, a bridge to that other realm. How I wanted a harp like this for my own, but there was no way I could afford it. As it turned out, I could. The cost matched — exactly — the amount available for me to spend from a faculty fund at the seminary where I am employed. So Al Winters hand carved and strung a large and beautiful harp for me and delivered it to my door the day after my birthday, as semester break began. Spring flowed into summer. My Celtic harp and I were one. Song after song came rippling forth in an outpouring of praise, quantum songs from a quantum Spirit falling afresh on me.

I know my brother had something to do with arranging this for me. Death is one of those thin places where spirits pass between two worlds unseen and unobstructed with a certain amount of ease. The window of vulnerability left open in those who are left behind allows the spirit world free rein until that window closes as we move on with our lives. What Bob could not put into words or do for me this side of the veil has been reversed forever. He helped me again when I was anguishing over the specifics of quantum physics. "You know what to do," I heard his spirit say to mine. "The words are there within you. Just write it your own way." Yes, big brother is watching. What a blessing for me.

A final story. I was preparing a biblical storytelling session for a course in liturgy and said to the Spirit I would use the first four narratives that came to mind. I admit this was a roundabout way of asking for inspiration, and in no time at all, I was set. When I arrived for class, I looked around the room and saw that participants included a woman in a wheelchair, who had a little dog; a woman who was completely paralyzed and strapped to a special chair; and a man next to her, who was attending to her. He was completely blind. For a moment, I stood there, stunned. Coincidentally, I had chosen the gospel accounts of the paralytic; the blind man, Bartimaeus; the woman who was unable to stand up straight; and the Canaanite woman who challenged Jesus when he suggested it was inappropriate to give family food to the dogs. It turned out to be the most relevant storytelling session I have ever had. When it came to the part about the dog — and this is the gospel truth — the little dog, whose name is Angel, stood up, put her paws on the storyteller's legs, and began to bark.

Life is full of incidents that interrupt the flow of events to leave something behind. Coincidence. Synchronicity. Incidents attributed to coincidental grace. Such are the fingerprints of the Spirit touching our lives unexpectedly, facilitating connections that take us by surprise.

The Spirit's manifestations are more easily discernible to those who savor serendipity, delight in spontaneity, are quick to bend the rules. Like fireflies on a summer night, flashes of enlightenment, now here, now there, illuminate our landscape with refreshing interventions, as Spirit heightens our awareness and suspends our disbelief.

Daily, quantum Spirit is revealed through multiple manifestations to ordinary folk like us. Once we are aware of this, once we learn to identify the calling card of the Spirit, we will experience the Sacred in ways we never have before. The spirit of the living God is eager to communicate with us, ready to co-create with us, reaches out to connect with us and to connect us to one another.

Coincidence is characteristic of quantum spirituality. It shows us how the world around us looks through a quantum lens.

Creation

Everyone creates. Something. Somehow. It is our nature, this instinctive urge to conceive and to conceptualize and to continually bring to birth. The divine Creator's gift of life is mirrored in and manifested through our own creativity. We bring to term, bring to fruition, bring to the fore as we bring to life the full spectrum of whatever it takes to be freely and fully human. Just about everything we have and a whole lot of what we do each day reflect a creative touch of one kind or another. Ourselves, our space, our public place are billboards for the images that we ourselves create.

To be creative means to midwife order out of chaos. Professional artists know that the creative force flowing out from them takes on a life of its own that affects them intensely as it moves into the world. For those of us who dance in the fields of imagination and intuition, feel life before we comprehend it and are driven to express how we feel, creativity is the breath of fresh air that energizes and restores us, the place that we come home to after a rough ride in reality, a friend at the bend in the road. It is a way of being in the world that satisfies and sustains us, a lens that adds a layer of meaning to our run-of-the-mill routine.

It is often difficult for imaginative people, who are known to push the envelope when it comes to new ideas, to function within frameworks that put us in a box. It is always stressful to submit the results of our creative process for review and regulation by those who go by the rules.

I remember when I first started writing music for the liturgy. It was at the close of Vatican II. Before we could sing on Sunday in our chapel in Philadelphia, I had to submit what I had written to the Archdiocesan Music Commission in order to get their approval. This was, after all, the church's introduction to the English language following centuries of Latin. They couldn't allow just anyone to mess with the sacred texts.

The change went into effect on the First Sunday of Advent and I was ready for it. I sent my settings of the Sunday Proper to the local authorities. Permission to use it was granted, but very reluctantly. I submitted the music for the Second Sunday, although my heart wasn't in it. Their phone call made it clear to me that granting permission to use my settings was about to come to an end. "Leave it to the professionals," their representative said to me. Actually, I was one, but that was beside the point. "Can't wait that long," I said to him. "We have to sing on Sunday." I was told to return to the Latin, that it would take years before an appropriate setting would be approved.

What followed marks the beginning of a paradigm shift for me and is replete with paradox. I was reprimanded. "Your chant has a beat to it. There is no meter in chant." I was told to stop writing music for liturgy, to leave it to those who know what they are doing. "Don't send us anything more." I hung up feeling defeated, but only for a while. Of course my chant was metrical. The rhythmic accent of the English language is different than Latin chant. Because I had studied and sung the Gregorian chant for years, I knew exactly what I was doing. This was a new creation that had arrived ahead of the rules. I stopped asking for permission, but I kept on writing music. When Advent ended, I moved away from chant and picked up a guitar. Spirit gave me a new sound as I sang into the universe songs of praise from the heart. We can thank the Archdiocesan Office for "Joy is like the Rain."

To create means to do something different, to welcome into the world what has not been here before. The creative act itself is not meant to intimidate or threaten what is already there, although it often ends up that way, because some can't handle this *and* that but only this *or* that. I came up against this often as the church struggled to adjust to changes it failed to anticipate. Many, however, welcomed the new approaches to music and liturgy and wanted to learn more about them.

Members of my community and I introduced a ministry to facilitate this process, one that would eventually make its way around the world. One day, early on, we were asked to present a concert in a Catholic church in Canada. We were already out of the habit, but it hadn't been for long. The event had been planned for the children who attended the parish school. As we watched them enter the pews that filled the massive gothic structure, the parish priest walked past us, went up the steps to the tabernacle, removed the Sacred Species, and carried it out of the church. We felt the accusation hanging ice cold in the air. Beware of nuns in lay clothing, carrying guitars. As pastor he felt a responsibility to protect the Real Presence from sacrilegious behavior, which meant to him folk music in the sanctuary, a strange way to welcome visitors from the United States.

We were well into our concert when one of my sisters nudged me. "Don't look now," she whispered, "but I saw the confessional curtain move. He's hiding in the box." Indeed, he was, and every now and then, we saw him peek through the curtain. I've always wondered if our words and songs ever had an impact on him, and if one day he too was able to break out of his box. When we reminisce about those times, we remember a priest's determination to save the Body and Blood of Jesus from a group of singing nuns. He tried to take Jesus out of the church, but Jesus stayed and sought and received sanctuary in our hearts.

It is hard work to bring to birth. Ask any woman in labor. Yet it is worth the effort, the blood, sweat, and tears, the preparation, concentration, and determination, when finally one delivers, whether baby, book, dissertation, or the fulfillment of a dream. We look with admiration at an architectural treasure and seldom think of what went into laying the foundations, yet all the wonders of the world began with a single brick, or an isolated inspiration, or a whisper in the wind.

Think about that for a moment. Perhaps too much is made of finished products and project outcomes, too little attention paid to the creativity of the process. The world in which we live today captivates us with its cleverness and an avalanche of things. We can become so enamored with the ingenuity of others that we doubt the value of accomplishments coming forth from the likes of us. Pick up a pair of knitting needles, a paintbrush, a garden hoe, or something else that speaks to you. Feel the satisfaction of knit and purl, the color purple, the transformation of seed to flower, and reawaken the urge within to co-create with God.

We are always creating, whether or not we know it, adding extra to ordinary, whether or not it feels like anything extraordinary to us. We need to be more intentional if we hope to have an influence on what the world will be like tomorrow. If we want a just and peaceful world, we will have to create it.

Create space that reflects the characteristics of a global village, where diversity and neighborliness and acceptance are the norm. Make room at your table and in your heart for a multitude of perspectives, so that those who arrive as stranger will be able to depart as friend.

Create a climate where those you love and all whom you encounter are free to be themselves with you, free to stretch their wings and fly beyond the limitations they or others have imposed. Be generous with compassion and encouragement and support.

Create opportunities that will eventually make a difference for an individual, for society, for our beloved planet. Don't second-guess the value of the tiniest initiative. At home, at church, in synagogue or mosque, in a support group or in the workplace, intend to make a difference through your presence, and you will.

The creative process is where we can give form to what we are feeling and be who we really are. For me it has been my respite on a long road to freedom, a portal into a quantum universe and paradoxology.

> To whom shall we go when we feel lost,
> when we've burned the bridges we have crossed,
> when horizons shift and the way ahead
> leads into a world uninterpreted.
> To whom shall we go?
> To whom shall we go?
> Spirit of the Living God, our lives evolve in You,
> wherever we are, whatever we do.
>
> To whom shall we go when on our own,
> when we're living lives we have outgrown,
> when our faith is firm, but it's not the same:

it no longer fits in a finite frame.
To whom shall we go?
To whom shall we go?
Spirit of the Living God, our lives evolve in You,
wherever we are, whatever we do.

To whom shall we go in times of stress,
when we're forced to face our helplessness,
when we've given all and are asked for more,
when we wish things could be as they were before.
To whom shall we go?
To whom shall we go?
Spirit of the Living God, our lives evolve in You,
wherever we are, whatever we do.[32]

When we align ourselves with the Spirit through any act of creation, even the most mundane, we witness to the creative force that fills the universe. We witness to Divinity welling up and spilling over from deep inside of us.

Eyewitnesses to the Resurrection of Jesus were drawn into a new way of seeing, a new way of being in the world in and through the Spirit.

Today we are "I"-witnesses to the living, loving Spirit of God inherent in all creation. We incarnate how to be in the world in the way that Jesus intended, a more fully inclusive way to which he bore witness with his life and death and that which followed after.

Intuition. Imagination. Inspiration. Incarnation. Insight. Intention. Inclusion. These are gifts we can call upon as I-witnesses today.

I witness to the Spirit of God by being faithful to the call of the Spirit, no matter what the cost.

I witness to the Spirit of God when I live as God intended, open and responsive to the invitations of grace.

I witness to the Spirit of God through every act of creation that reaches out and welcomes in, gives and is forgiving.

I witness to the Spirit of God when I transcend traditional boundaries to bring to those outside the circle gifts of compassion and peace.

I witness to the Spirit of God when I trust that which I cannot see, listen to what the heart hears, give voice to that which is given to me and live my life accordingly.

I witness to the Spirit of God when I embody the wisdom of God and am open to everyone.

I witness to the Spirit of God by loving everyone.

Celebration

In the beginning
before and beyond when and where
our own particular beginning began
INFINITY
ETERNITY
ENERGY
MYSTERY
GOD

In the beginning
of our beginning
our universe
our planet Earth
SPIRIT
SPONTANEITY

SERENDIPITY
SHALOM

water
water everywhere
oceans, geysers, rivers, rain
giving birth
saturate Earth

air
gust, wind, storm
breath of life
invisible form
howling, swirling, blowing away
what cannot be captive
any way

fire
synchronistic light
sun by day, moon at night
meet, merge, move apart
every dawn a new start
for the seasons
of the heart

Earth
wakens, wondrously
seed, plant, bush, tree
flower and flaunt continuously
with infinite diversity
a single cell
the right milieu
profusion of forms
old and new

emerging and evolving:
fin, wing, hoof, claw
humanity
multiplicity
synchronicity
awe

In the beginning
our beginning:
SOUL

WHOLE

SACRED

ONE

DIVERSITY

DIVINITY

GOD

O insatiable Mystery
I in You and You in me
paradox
paradoxology

❧❧❧

Praise God, heaven and Earth!
Sing praise from the ends of the universe,
to the frontiers of space and beyond.
Sing praise all you nations, all you people, all creation.
Sun and moon, planets and stars,
light lamps in celebration.
Oceans and seas, send forth waves of joy-filled jubilation.
Winds, dance across the plains
and blow, blow, blow away the clouds of desolation.
Trees of the forest, clap your hands.

Mountains and hills and desert sands,
lift up your voice as the song expands.
Rivers and streams, dance in delight,
from the dawn of day through the dark of night.
Flowering fields, frost and rain,
sing your song, sing it again.
Fish, butterflies, birds, bees,
from the mammoth beast to the least of these:
all that lives, all that is, sing your praise to God.

Spirit of God, stir within your creation.
Make us aware of the gifts you instill.
Open us to a new revelation:
fulfill the earth, bring it birth, and blow where you will.
Blow, blow, blow till I be but breath of the Spirit
blowing in me.[33]

There is something about a candle.
A microcosm of cosmic light.
Our kinship with a distant star.
Prelude to the rising sun
when the wavering voice within us says
there will be no morning after.
Promise to oneself at night
not to be afraid of the dark.
Bolt of light in a violent storm.
Vigil lamp in memory of a loved one not returning.
Radiant witness to life beyond life.
Beacon illuminating our way.
Glimmer of hope.
Ray of relief.

A burning passion to never give up
but to live life regardless.
When feeling overwhelmed
with grief or regret,
when restless
or afraid,
let a candle's illumination
touch your turbulent heart.
There is something primal about fire.
There is mystery in the flame's ability
to ignite a spark within us
and link us to worlds beyond ourselves.
There is something about a candle.
Flickering light.
Rippling light.
Healing light.
Holy light.
Sometimes the only comfort we know
is a candle in the wind.[34]

All Earth's people, clap your hands.
Join in celebration.
Weave a web of ancestral lands
into a new creation.
Soon now, hope will come of age.
Start the circle dances.
We are poised to turn a page
and change our circumstances.
The wind in the willow has understood
and whispers wisdom to us:

all that is gracious and all that is good
will enter us and renew us.
Ours is the bounty of planet Earth.
Savor it and share it.
Ensure there will be enough of worth
for our children to inherit.
Now is the time to act as one.
Myriad are the reasons.
The age of the Spirit has begun.
Celebrate its seasons.
The One through whom we came to be,
in whom our spirit dances,
can forgive iniquity
and give us second chances.[35]

❧❧❧

Light a candle in your heart.
Show love from within.
Tell retaliation to depart.
Let the healing of the world begin.[36]

Chapter 8

Gifts of a Quantum Spirit

In a quantum universe, everything is gift of the Spirit. Life. Breath. The world we live in. Family. Friends. Our future. Even those moments marring our memories of the past, for the forces of death and destruction are not always demonic. Divinity often visits us in our shadows and our storms. Whatever God gives has value, although we may have to wait a while before we comprehend the wisdom some events were meant to convey.

In a world where everything is a gift, we tend to take for granted the blessings we depend upon and are slow to give thanks to our Sacred Source for all that we have and are. As life begins to reflect the dynamic effects of a quantum influence, new needs will arise and new gifts will be given in response to our changing times. The Holy Spirit will guide our efforts to make a graced transition from all that has been to whatever lies ahead in the world that is emerging. As we enter into this process, we will become more and more aware that genuine spirituality is an integral part of our natural world and the unfolding of our lives.

Seven gifts of the Spirit taken from quantum theory seem particularly appropriate as steppingstones into a spirituality shaped by a quantum universe. These gifts are Relativity, Uncertainty, Probability, Complementarity,

Nonlocality, Synchronicity, and Change. As we read and reflect on these seven gifts and wrestle with their implications, by ourselves or with a circle of friends, the following points for reflection may facilitate our efforts to integrate them into a spirituality of our own.

• Name one way this gift has already been visible in your life.

• Recall an incident in which this gift might have helped to clarify a situation that was difficult to understand.

• If this gift were an integral part of your own spirituality, how would it help you live with integrity in our rapidly changing times?

Relativity

Everything is relative. Then again, it's not. These two positions, pro and con, sum up this reflection.

In the world where I grew up, it had to be one or the other. This isn't so any longer. It doesn't have to be this *or* that. In fact it can be this *and* that. Opposites are not mutually exclusive in a quantum universe. At least that's what they say, those who know about such things. Long after he published his groundbreaking Theory of Relativity, Albert Einstein explained it in terms anyone can understand. "When a man sits with a pretty girl for an hour, it seems like a minute. But let him sit on a hot stove for a minute and it's longer than an hour. That's relativity."[37]

Reality is relative to experience and conditioned by perception. The way we see or experience something is how it really is, even if only to us. Consequently, eyewitness testimony is relatively unreliable. People seeing the same thing can arrive at different conclusions because of extenuating circumstances. Our mood, perhaps, or personality or angle of perception or any number of subjective factors can add a dimension of relativity to reality. What you see is what you get, and that may deviate from fact. The same can be said of individuals within a given system. For example, I am a Christian. A lot of people are, yet what this means to each one of us and how we perceive the relationship between our faith and our fidelity differs widely among us. There are many religious paths giving rise to countless variations. From a quantum perspective all are legitimate, for in a quantum universe deviation is the norm.

Relativity is not a concept the institutional church condones. Christianity through the centuries has been dominated by absolutes. All one needs to know or believe is absolutely clear and absolutely certain. Creeds and canons codify. Commandments control. Choice is unequivocal. Thou shalt or thou shalt not. There can be no discussion and no ambivalence. From this perspective Christian religion is the opposite of quantum, but to state this so definitively is to miss the quantum point of not necessarily either/or.

Ironically, Christianity is permeated with realities that are both this and that and is steeped in traditions based on believing unbelievable things. A virgin conceives and bears a child. That child, a man of miracles, is both human and divine. His Body and Blood are with us in the elements of the Eucharist, where the energy of a past event is experienced here and now. This is quantum reality. Relativity also enters with those who are outside the Christian faith, and even with some within it who say that, for them, these tenets are not absolutely and unequivocally the facts of life.

There are many quantum aspects to the life and legacy of Jesus that suddenly appear, like stars in the sky, when we look through a quantum lens. Relativity is one. It thrives beneath an avalanche of absolutes associated with him. Look, for example, at the metaphors that weave in and out of his story. We are so familiar with metaphors that it may come as a surprise to hear of their quantum qualities. Metaphors top the charts when it comes to relativity.

A metaphor is and isn't. It is simultaneously this and that. Jesus manifested a quantum Spirit by habitually turning to metaphors to express what could not be put into words, instantly forging a link between the temporal and the eternal, between himself and creation, between himself and us. Jesus the vine and we the branches (John 15:1–11). This is a grace-laden metaphor for me. The relationship between Jesus and me is like a vine to its branches, integral and sustaining, yet I do not take this literally from a biological standpoint, because I know, in the physical world, we are not twigs, but people. This is relativity. So is the fact that this image, so full of life and meaning for me, is not for everyone. Meaning is linked to perception, which in this case takes form under the influence of faith.

Jesus confronted perception head on when he posed these tantalizing questions. "Who do people say that I am?" "Who do you say that I am?" (Mark 8:27–29). Whoever people thought Jesus was, whoever his disciples thought he was, appeared to have a life of its own. The perception of others often did not coincide with his self-perception. Some thought he was otherworldly. Others said he was demonic. Still others felt he was a threat and misinterpreted his intentions. Many were devoted to him for reasons of their own. Perception and misperception, paradoxical aspects of relativity, forge a bond between Jesus and us through a shared humanity. How do we see Jesus? How do we see others? How do others see us? How do we see ourselves? What Jesus means to us today depends on who we perceive him to be.

With Jesus there are times when this incongruity between reality and perception reflects a cosmic dimension. Whenever we feed the hungry, we are told, or minister to the suffering, it is Jesus whom we serve. The bodies of those who are in need are said to be his body. This is quantumstuff, and we have to learn how to live it, not just on occasion, but every day of our lives. When was the last time we saw Jesus in someone who was asking for alms? Or standing in line at a shelter? Or on the way to jail? I forget to make that connection when I step away from my computer where this manuscript is in process, or at the end of my morning prayer. Theoretical assent is one thing, but theory is of no earthly use if we don't put it into practice. Jesus is made manifest though concrete works of mercy. His spirit, a holy spirit, inhabits and infuses all incarnate realities. I saw him up close this afternoon, hunched over in a wheelchair at a nearby nursing home, the embodiment of despair. It was my brother Jesus in the skin of my sibling, Jack. All of a sudden, word became flesh, living here among us, waiting there for me.

Relativity is integral to who we are and the way we orient ourselves in the world. Relative does not mean irrelevant, or irresponsible, which is often the position of those who are caught up in absolutes. As we become more comfortable with relativity, we will start to see its blessing side in the unfolding of our lives. If things don't turn out as we had hoped, it may not mean we failed but that things failed to go our way. It is then we need to remind ourselves that God's ways are not our ways. A relationship we thought was forever, but instead ended relatively soon, may have given us just what we needed to move on with the rest of our lives. Life can be relatively peaceful or relatively hard to endure, depending on how we approach the ups and downs that we incur. Our choices are seldom black and white but, as my digital printer says, multiple shades of gray.

Why, then, this compulsive preference for the absolute? The drive is deep within us to be absolutely perfect, to be absolutely right. God alone is Absolute. Everything else is relative — the paths we take, the homage we make, our religious rites and ritual roles and sacramental behaviors, our theories and theologies, sacred texts and sacred spaces. All knowledge of God is relative. God alone is absolutely certain of that which is definitive of God.

Spirituality thrives on relativity because it is rooted in life, and so much of life is relative. Just to be is to be diverse in every imaginable way, and in ways we cannot imagine, making the notion of rigidity inconceivable. There are so many options to any one thing, so many paths as we move toward a goal, so many approaches relative to whatever we intend. One wonders how we got so stuck in our inflexibilities, setting our castles of sand in stone, only to watch them crumble and drift away with the shifting tide. If reality is relative to what we see, then the more diverse the lenses we use in gaining a perspective and the wider our range of perception, the wiser we will be.

Once we comprehend the relativity of our structures and inflexible assumptions and can separate what is meaningful from all the clutter that is not, an inner peace will arise and spread like the sun on a summer day. Then a response to perennial questions will suddenly satisfy. What is life? It is what it is. Who are we? We are who we are. What of the future? What will be will be. We will sense on some deep level that we will just have to live with that.

Uncertainty

Who doesn't prefer a sure thing? Who wouldn't try to hedge their bets when up against the odds? We want absolute certainty anytime we can get it, will do anything to ensure it, are positively convinced that without it we simply can't go on. Most of us are products of an era of certitude. We have been conditioned by guarantees. I'm still amazed that warranties today aren't worth the paper they are printed on, a clear indication among many others that something of substance has changed. We live in an age of uncertainty where we still make lots of promises, but there are no guarantees.

Doubt in that dominating age of certitude was like the gorilla in the living room. Nearly everyone sensed that something was amiss, but no one would admit it. In religious circles during those days, doubt was akin to committing a sin. You weren't supposed to have it. Shame on you, if you doubted an authoritative word.

When I was young I discovered a devotion to the Sacred Heart of Jesus. Whoever received Communion on the first

Friday of the month for nine consecutive months would go straight to heaven when they died. Jesus promised, the pamphlet said, so do it. And I did. But then I began to wonder. Had I been attentive? Were my prayers sincere? Was what I had done good enough? A sense of my own unworthiness to be blessed with that divine guarantee filled me with uncertainty, so I did the nine first Fridays again, and then again, just to be sure. The truth is, I was never convinced that such a simple practice was sufficient for a free pass into paradise. Did I really believe that no matter how the rest of my life turned out, heaven was assured? It was one thing to doubt myself, but a scandal to question a promise that Jesus was said to have made. Yet as I scolded myself for doubting, deep within an unwavering trust in the loving forgiveness of Jesus insisted he would not hold it against me if that promise turned out to be true.

Doubt is the nemesis of absolute certitude, which is why it is forbidden when blind obedience is required. Not so in an age of uncertainty, where doubt is not only acceptable, it is legitimate, even though it may leave us feeling insecure because we can no longer be sure of what had been absolutely certain.

Try to remember, if you can, a time when you first began to doubt something or someone. Was it Santa Claus? Or the tooth fairy? Or the necessity of eating fish on Friday? Or the existence of a place called Limbo? Or its mysterious disappearance? How did you feel about questioning what you had always assumed to be true? Guilty? Betrayed?

Doubt in an age where all is in flux is ephemeral and fleeting and can be counted on to return. As soon as one doubt is assuaged, another begins to form. Doubt is characteristic of rationality. We need to make friends with it.

We need to give ourselves permission to be skeptical or inquisitive about things we have always taken for granted as unassailable truth.

Before cosmological enlightenment, our universe was compared to a machine made up of many parts, or a clock with its separate elements performing essential functions with constancy and precision. Everything had a cause that led directly to its outcome. This relationship of cause and effect meant things were predictable. One had absolute assurance that what was not known at the present time would eventually be revealed, because everything was a consequence of some prior cause. This mechanistic era, an age of reason, became an age of certainty, where perplexities were challenges to analyze and resolve.

The Newtonian worldview, as it came to be known, symbolizes a particular way of being in the world, and it continues to insinuate itself in how we order our lives. So much of our lived reality still reflects a mechanical model consisting of movable parts within a hierarchical structure. It is still fairly easy, therefore, to remove a weak link or reconfigure what is deemed dysfunctional, but a clockwork consistency cannot be guaranteed.

Without this dependability, we are no longer confident that everything will be okay. What is gone is an assurance that those structures essential to stability and some kind of continuity will be there when we get up in the morning, that there will be a job to go to, a paycheck the family depends upon, medical care in a crisis, a roof over our head. Systemically, a façade of sorts suggests we are overreacting, but we, out here in the trenches, insist it is otherwise. The world as we know it is falling apart and there seems to be no way to fix it. Those tools that enabled us to function, such as predictability and inevitability, are relics of the past. As we move into the future, as stabilizing supports continue to erode, we need to face the facts of change and come to terms with uncertainty. We have to stop clinging to those remnants of certitude that are no longer relevant and stop swimming against the tide. It is time to move away from a presumption of invulnerability toward an acceptance of those insecurities a quantum universe implies.

One of the ways to begin this psychological transition is by demythologizing such pillars of the past as predictability. Life has never been predictable. When were we ever 100 percent sure that things would go our way? We may look back on what has been, but it never was what we thought it was, so it can't be that way again. It doesn't matter that our five-year plans allowed us to make projections. We tend to forget how many times those plans had to be redone. Unpredictability darts in and out of our lives as slippery as an eel, and when we cannot corner it or find a way to control it, we pretend it isn't there. All the while predictability is sustained by a myth of our own making. When we stop paying homage to it in those places where it has ceased to exist, the dynamics of a quantum universe will begin to make more sense to us, and we will discover the graced potential that comes with being unsure.

We need to remember we are not going through this time of transition alone. A firm foundational certitude undergirds our ambiguities. It is the conviction that the Spirit of God remains our guarantee. Faith in a quantum Spirit will sustain us through the turbulence generated by a sea of uncertainty. Once we cross over to the other side, we can begin to access some of the strengths and positive potential inherent in what we presently fear. I see these words every day on my desk: "You cannot discover new oceans unless you have the courage to lose sight of the shore." Uncertainty goes hand in hand with relativity. Both set firm foundations on precariously shifting sand. Quantum Spirit will help us find a kind of stability there.

Certain aspects of uncertainty resonate with me. For instance, I like surprises. The unexpected holds within it a fragment of mystery. There may be times when it doesn't deliver, when it leaves me halfway to a high before I come crashing down. But then there is anticipatory suspense where you don't know what will happen next, but you know it will be worth waiting for, like at the end of Advent, when you feel the spirit of Christmas rising with the solstice moon. Part of me prefers this kind of uncertainty, this kind of fluidity, and the feeling of freedom that comes when life is revealed as it unfolds.

One of the close companions of uncertainty is risk. To be at risk is synonymous with living on the edge, which is often debilitating, but may also be exhilarating, as when one is on the crest of a wave or in free fall through time and space before the parachute opens. Risk implies some unknown peril may be lurking just ahead, whether on the road that must be taken, the path we opt for on a whim, or out on the water that once seemed so inviting from the shore. In any case, one has to let go and be ready for adventure or for potential disaster, be willing to enter into a daring encounter with the unknown.

Risk-taking is heroic. Sometimes it is inevitable. Going on patrol in a war zone, carrying an unconscious child out of a burning building, performing life-saving surgery, whistle blowing when a lot is at stake and the odds of winning are zero, knowing you are dangerously close to pitching your tent on the street. Some risk is unacceptable, no matter how uncertain the times. There are far too many children today whose very lives are at risk. The certainty of their uncertainty is a byproduct of our indifference, and for this, we should all be ashamed. It is only our faith in a compassionate God who moves people to compassionate deeds that assures us this too will change.

My prayer in these uncertain times is, "O Holy One, I believe. Help my unbelief." The uncertainty of belief in an uncertain age may already be pandemic, but so is a countermovement of faith firmly rooted in the Divine.

Probability

I must confess I remain hooked on dreaming the impossible dream, on overcoming every barrier that stands in the way of harmonious international relationships heralding peace and good will among all. I think perhaps I have always had a passion for possibilities. Quantumstuff kicks it up a notch to a penchant for probabilities. This still leaves something to be desired, but it moves us well beyond maybe. If the possible becomes probable, then we're already halfway there. I used to say, "When one has faith, anything is possible." Now I say, "In and through the Spirit, everything is probable." Probability is at the core of quantum spirituality because it is characteristic of a quantum universe.

The laws of quantum physics are expressed in terms of probabilities that may or may not happen. Like tickets in a lottery, there is no way of predicting which combination will come to the fore, yet there is usually someone out there who has the winning hand. Whether one takes a chance on peace or gambles on prosperity, the probability of success keeps hope alive in the pragmatist and the dreamer, and that is why exuberance survives the deprivations of despair. For those who are optimistic, relief is right around the corner. Something great is going to happen any minute now. You can almost hear the good news echo from the stubs you have discarded. You nearly won the lottery. You were just a digit away.

Probabilities exist as potentialities until they are actualized. Worlds of unrealized potential throughout the universe and throughout our lives await an influx of probable cause. A mother looks at her newborn baby and sees the potential of her loving heart fully realized. She imagines the possibilities for the life that is just beginning, weighs the probability of her child becoming either this or that, and rejoices moment by moment in the baby's here and now.

For a child every discovery is actualized potential, and more often then not it is accompanied by unrestrained delight. That may shift during adolescence, when the full force of reality is confronted at every turn. If only we could hold on to the feeling of bliss in our becoming and not get tangled up in games that others would have us play. All too soon there will come a time when we no longer get excited about exploring opportunities or exercising our options. We awake one day to the realization that we have untapped potential and we are running out of time, that some gifts have yet to materialize and probably never will. During such moments we need to remember that each of us carries within us a galaxy of probabilities waiting to be fulfilled. We are never too old and it is never too late to ignite a spark that will tip probability toward actualization. We can do this again and again.

Quantum physics describes matter as a wave of probability that has the innate capacities of both particle and wave. The wave function collapses to allow the particle to be observed. Otherwise, the wave is the means of mobility and momentum. The normative state of matter, therefore, is not particle, but wave.

We who are human put a lot of effort into functioning in the opposite way. For instance, here in America, individuality and particularity are decisively the norm. We are more like particles than waves. Time and again the whole is achieved through an amalgamation of parts. To gain momentum we increase the numbers of those who are involved. Statistics seem to be everything, because individuals are an important part of failure or success. A surge of troops in a battle zone, an increase in prison populations, the gerrymandering of districts in order to influence an election underscore the role of populations in protecting the status quo. Too many illegal aliens results in a tightly regulated border, and too few votes in favor of benefits for the disadvantaged allows us to retain our systemic bias against the poor.

Materialism and going into debt appear to be national obsessions, whereby a few are able to amass an inordinate amount of funds and favors to the detriment of us all. We need to spend time studying the symbiotic relationship between particle and wave. The selfish and self-centered can no longer be allowed to control the masses by means of global monopolies if people and planet are to survive long enough to actualize their potential.

There is raw power and pent up potency packed within a wave. We can feel it spilling over in a happening or a movement that has suddenly gained momentum; feel energy ricochet through us in a jam-packed stadium cheering for a team; feel it pull us to our feet at the end of a stellar performance; feel it rise like the phoenix when an underdog overturns the tables on the way to victory. The dynamic forces of nature — the wind, the surf, the rolling thunder, migrating birds, and monsoon rains — come and go in waves. The process whereby systemic change reaches a tipping point also undulates like a wave, beginning quietly, gaining force, rolling in and up and over and out, affecting all, changing all, as it wipes away accretions and assumptions and assertions in a thrust of urgency.

That's how it was in the explosive wake of the Second Vatican Council. Age-old particularities of liturgical rites and religious orders were swept away in a wave of reform. Successful liberation movements are those that are able to catch the wave and ride it to its conclusion. When a critical mass stood together singing "We Shall Overcome," the civil rights movement reached the tipping point and there was nothing that could stop it. I never thought I would see a woman priest in the Roman Catholic tradition, until the day I met one; or an African American president, until a candidate's presidential campaign asked for my support.

We are awash in waves of probability that are cresting everywhere. What is probable can become actual in the twinkling of an eye. Waves are impervious to convention and impossible to restrain. Waves are always on the verge of unleashing something new.

Science speaks of probability in terms of "tendencies." On the subatomic level, matter does not exist definitively at designated places but shows "tendencies to exist." Events do not occur at predictable times and in predictable ways, or in predictable places, but show "tendencies to occur." These tendencies are probabilities that take the form of waves.

The phrase "tendency to occur" tips the balance of probability a whole lot closer to "about to happen," giving us language and imagery to substantiate our hope for peace on earth and a meaningful life for all. A tendency is an inclination, and we are inclined as a nation, and in most cases individually, to see that justice does prevail, to put food on the table of the hungry in our midst, to find adequate housing for people living on the street.

Liberation theology speaks of God's tendency to favor the poor, according to biblical tradition. Such an inclination, or bias, is much more than an intermittent leaning in a particular direction. It is a disposition to act, which means being permanently disposed to behave in ways that benefit others, particularly the disadvantaged. It is the actualization of the tendency to do good to others, the tendency to live peacefully, the tendency to love one another as God loves us. How fortunate we are to be inundated with tendencies such as these. Within us and all around us are blessings with tendencies to occur, good deeds with tendencies to exist. The impossible dream becomes probable in a quantum universe.

As we garner a new vocabulary here for quantum spirituality, we shift from a worldview of possibility to one of probability. What is possible is conceivable, but it is not probable; therefore, it is unlikely to occur. What is probable may not be certain, but there is a good chance it will happen; and because it is reasonable to expect it to happen, it is likely to occur.

In a world teeming with probabilities, there are ample opportunities for good things to exist. It is our responsibility to ensure that this is so.

Complementarity

Niels Bohr was on holiday in 1927 when suddenly he realized that the wave/particle duality was the key to understanding the new quantum physics. His principle of complementarity changed the perception of reality within the scientific community. The rest of the world, however, has been slow to get on board. We are starting to pay attention now to what his discovery was all about. I was on sabbatical in 2007 when I finally realized that complementarity is central to quantum spirituality. Here is the factual pinnacle from which I took that quantum leap.

In the subatomic world fundamental elements of matter exhibit the mutually exclusive behavior of both particle and wave. In scientific experiments, one can observe the properties of either particle or wave depending on what one expects to see. Although particle and wave behaviors can never be visible at the same time, both are essential. This is what is meant by complementarity. Previously, in classical science, an entity would have to be one or the other, either particle or wave, because a particle has mass, or substance, and a wave does not. However, the new science insists that it is not one *or* the other, but one *and* the other, no matter how illogical or how impossible this may seem. At the heart of a scientific explanation of our quantum universe lies this inability to fully understand its fundamental premises.

Much to my surprise, I find the concept of complementarity fairly easy to accept, even though I can't comprehend it. There are two reasons for this. First, as a person of faith, I am in a committed relationship with a divine being, who is known and yet not known. This means I live a life that is dedicated to what I can't fully grasp. It is common today to insist that theology is "faith seeking understanding."[38] Yet I am a theologian who doesn't always seek to understand. I can embrace the cloud of unknowing. I delight in mystery.

The second reason has to do with my cosmological sign. Gemini means that I carry a cosmic polarity within me. The energies of the Gemini twins ensure that I live intimately with a complementarity of my own. I am constantly bouncing back and forth between dual orientations that tend to nudge me in opposite directions a good deal of the time. The part of me that prefers intuition is the one who writes from the gut and not from the place that knows what is coming next; the one whose journey of the heart has no clear destination, no set expectations; the one who simply enjoys what is experienced along the way. The other one, on the other hand, has all the earmarks of a need for clarity and control. That side would rather not wing it, is wondering when I will finish this book, would read every book on the planet before writing a single word.

This vacillation back and forth is augmented by another dance between right brain and left brain, which takes the physical shape of imagination and concretization, theophany and theology, uncertainty and certitude, poetry and pedagogy, a yearning to let things be that is too often over-ridden by a list of things to do. For most of my life I would find myself periodically dominated by one side or the other. I was either a singer of songs or the resident academic, a free and unfettered spirit or the responsible adult, until a quantum immersion gave rise to a deeper integration. I am moving beyond a preeminence of one over another in favor of a blend of the strengths of both, with more wholistic outcomes.

The ping-pong approach of a zodiac sign is a movement of cosmic proportions in which the universe participates. When I look a little more closely at the natural world around me, I see symbiotic relationships and complementary partnerships flourishing everywhere. The inclination of life is not toward separation or isolation but rather toward a fruitful togetherness, where the distinctiveness of each entity remains sacrosanct. Complementarity is not an arbitrary pairing, nor is it superfluous. It is, by definition, a necessary interrelationship — a complementary interrelationship — in which two parts complete each other, mutually making up for what is lacking in one or the other when otherwise on their own. Isn't this what best friends are for, or what most people are looking for in a partner or a mate? Could this be why opposites attract with such intensity? I often see how certain people complement one another, and through that interchange of energy everyone is enriched.

A sense of completion or coming full circle to a place where one can feel at home in a relationship is also what we hope to find in a vocation or a career. Unfortunately, there is often dissatisfaction in the workplace. Whenever a job is just a job and what we do doesn't matter, when a place of employment is not a good fit, when market-driven priorities state we are all dispensable, it is hard to be enthusiastic about showing up in the morning. There are places, however, where the principle of complementarity seems solidly in place and waves of energy reveal that all participating partnerships are vital to the whole.

Complementarity may well be the cornerstone of our nation. A republic of states united around a commitment to core values, pledging liberty and justice for all the many and diverse cultures that lay claim to citizenship is a microcosm of the new world order, in theory, if not in fact. What we must avoid, however, are naïve attempts to package and export our principal ideals in ways that are despotic, for a quantum universe teaches us that transformative change is organic and happens from within. When we begin living up to our own grandiose expectations and practice more of what we preach, we will model the ways and means whereby other cultural collectives can choose to select what is best for them and the preservation of what they value.

The principle of complementarity also supports an educational model that is slowly gaining credence. It consists of learning circles where all are teachers and all are students who exchange information, build on experience, and honor what has been shared. Teaching and learning are no longer mutually exclusive. When this pedagogical principle finally reaches its tipping point, we will have learned how to listen to the wisdom in our midst. Ordinary people will tell of how we can be who we are called to be and do what our conscience compels us to do, and those who are in authority will help to make it so.

These seemingly impossible dreams are not vestiges of
the past, but present hopes, probability waves poised to
break upon us, living reminders that politics and spirituality are forever entwined. Spirituality is about what we
do, and also the way we do it, our personal and public expressions of our relationship with the Divine. The world
may be getting smaller, but its scope of concern is much
bigger than it has ever been before. What we essentially
hope for is that our desires and expectations complement
those of others, especially those who are different from
us, especially those who, together with us, would make
our world a better place for future generations.

Hope in a time when the vestiges of hope are in short
supply goes to the heart of what quantum spirituality is
about. The Spirit hovers over the void that once was filled
with believers, bringing forth from the ensuing chaos reason to go on living, even reasons to rejoice. The more we
open up to the energies of the universe, the home of a hallowed Presence, and the more disposed we are to respond
to its cosmic invitation, the more we will discover how our
own participation is an integral part of it all.

The particle/wave dilemma at the heart of quantum
theory permeates spirituality. It is mystery and miracle. It
is revelation of what lies deep within a reality we cannot
see. It is faith in a world beyond our world and countless incomprehensible moments we will never understand.
The quantum soul of the universe is the universal soul of
quantum spirituality. The sum of all particularity rides
its waves from one generation into and beyond the next.
The mystical and the prophetic, the temporal and the
eternal complement and bring to fulfillment those divine
intuitions genetically encoded in us.

Nonlocality

While I was in India visiting indigenous communities of Medical Mission Sisters, I stopped by the department of naturopathy in our hospital in Patna. "What is that?" I asked, pointing to a tray that held a number of very small vials. Annamah, who is one of our sisters, said that each of the vials held a follicle of hair taken from a former patient. These represented individuals who had completed their course of treatment and returned to their village homes. Periodically the hair was analyzed for any indication that their illness might have recurred. She said it was possible to assess the state of a person's health this way, even though the individual and the follicle of hair were no longer connected. That was my introduction to nonlocality.

Underlying this phenomenon is an aspect of quantum-stuff. John Bell published his theory of nonlocality in 1970, which provides mathematical proof for asserting that reality is nonlocal. This means that elements of nature do not have to be in the same locale in order to connect. For instance, two subatomic elements that once had interacted and are now separated by distance can reconnect again. That reconnection is instantaneous, no matter how far apart they are. In fact, an element here on Earth can link up with another in space with a velocity that exceeds the speed of light. Bell's theorem indicates that this is not an isolated incident but a universal principle, and that only a nonlocal model of reality corresponds with quantum facts.

Further speculation suggests that this nonlocal connection may be due to phase entanglement, which occurs when two systems interact and their energies intermingle. Once the systems separate, something of each remains in the other, leaving the two connected within the quantum realm. This quantum phase connection may well be the unifying principle underlying physical reality. As systems interact and intertwine in ever expanding circles, the potential for a wider innerconnectedness continues on. The implications of this are astounding. If an atom's sphere of influence extends well beyond a given locale, then a whole new range of possibilities or, more accurately, probabilities opens up for the world we live in, once we openly acknowledge the potential implicit here.

Our present global technology already substantiates this claim. At any time of the day or night we are instantly connected to friends, and even absolute strangers, via the Internet. With the click of a mouse, in the blink of an eye, we can call up information on just about anything, peruse archives, review merchandise, place an order, pay a bill, find a long lost relative or friend, complete a multitude of tasks — all without stepping away from the keyboard that connects us to our computer and to the world at large. The present generation takes this phenomenon for granted, while we who are remnants of the typewriter age still marvel at it all. Once when I sought technological assistance over the telephone, Henry answered the call. The source of the problem may be the storm that is in your area, he said. There is no storm here, I responded. He named the place, which is located just beyond our city limits. Henry was in India, and he knew long before I did that there was a storm in America, right around the corner from me, that might be affecting my computer. Then he proceeded step by step to help me solve my problem, speaking as though he were in the room, not thousands of miles away.

The notion of nonlocality is engulfing the planet in the form of a technological tidal wave, and implications for spirituality are following in its wake. For example, when it comes to prayer, people of faith have always known that prayer can be efficacious. Now some scientists also admit that prayer can be effective, that prayer is in fact "good medicine,"[39] that those for whom someone has prayed often reflect prayer's positive influence in the healing process, because a connection has been established across an expanse of space.

Scientific confirmation of prayer's validity does not speak to its basis in faith but to its quantum connection, its nonlocality, revealing yet another way in which our physical world and the world of the spirit intersect. Hospitals and medical centers are beginning to pay attention to the claims of energy medicine and wholistic healing, making it possible for patients to have access to Reiki, acupuncture, acupressure, and the healing effects of music.

Some will say that nonlocality is incompatible with Christianity. Not so, for a sense of nonlocality permeates the life of Jesus and our Christian faith. For instance, when the centurion in Capernaum pleaded with Jesus to cure his paralyzed servant, he asked him to do so from a distance, saying he was unworthy of having Jesus come to his home. "Say but the word," he insisted, "and my servant will be healed" (Matt. 8:8). Jesus complied, healing the servant instantaneously. Catholics repeat the centurion's words before receiving Holy Communion, linking across time and space all those who come to Jesus hoping to be healed.

Faith-based nonlocality is deeply rooted in the risen Christ and constitutive of our faith. The resurrection narratives insist that the one who died and was buried suddenly appeared among them, a phenomenon no one was able to explain and many refused to deny. Jesus the Jew had been transformed into a spiritual force no longer limited by locale, yet encountered locally. "Remember, I am with you always" (Matt. 28:20). This promise made by Jesus transcends the limits of the time and place in which the words were spoken. It is a lasting covenant, assuring a living presence anytime and anywhere. This is quantum spirituality and it is foundational to a new way of being in the world.

What does this mean for you and me? It means that when we take time to pray in the name of Jesus, he is there with us, just as he promised, in the fullness of his spirit. We cannot escape his presence, for the Spirit that connects us to him and to one another is the spirit of our everywhere God. Those who have gone before us remain present to us in spirit as well in what has been called a communion of saints that extends through the ages. A living nonlocal presence, experienced locally, extending globally, connects in spirit all people of faith in the spirit of the living God.

Christian spirituality has many similar elements of a quantum nature. We are simply less aware of them because of an overemphasis on the more didactic aspects associated with our faith. We need to start trusting our intuitive sense a whole lot more than we have in the past, for traces of an ancient, more universal wisdom are encoded in our DNA. Once we begin to take seriously the fact that whatever happens locally affects life at a distance, we can begin to bring about the changes for which we long. To give substance to that for which we hope — this is one of the outcomes of spirituality in a quantum universe. Of all the quantum gifts we can expect from a quantum Spirit, nonlocality has the capacity to radically change us all.

Synchronicity

For too long we have been out of synch with the rhythms of life on our planet. If what we cherish is to survive beyond the twenty-first century, then that will have to change.

I would imagine all of us have experienced at least once in our lifetime what it feels like to be completely in synch, as if we were one with the universe, as if there were no separation between our environment and ourselves. If so, we will remember the moment when an energy overwhelmed us and demolished our inhibitions, when we broke through our encapsulated self and could soar beyond our limits with no fear at all of falling. We were ageless. We could fly.

Being in synch feels like just about anything is possible, that the locus of our longing is right here within our reach. It is the bliss of going with the flow wherever the Spirit leads us, without a compass, without a plan, without any expectations. Is this how the wind feels as it goes on billowing where it will? And if indeed the wind cannot feel, are we sensory surrogates for it? To be one with the wind, the willow, the wave, if only for a little while, is to know what synchronicity is and to ache for it ever after.

Extraordinary moments of synchronicity arrive unanticipated and unannounced. They do not come very often, except to the fortunate few, to mystics and psychics, for instance, and twins, whose genetic connection results in simultaneous choices even when they are far apart. A more normative synchronicity permeates daily life. Who has not been mesmerized by the synchronized movement of a chorus line, an ensemble of ballerinas, swimmers performing in unison, bands marching in a parade, a school of fish, a flock of birds, a swarm of bees surging ahead and never once colliding? Who can resist the magnetic pull of jazz, the blues, a cathedral choir, the fiery force of flamenco?

Invisible vibrations underlying the melody, harmony, and rhythm of music attract and unify. As one who sings new songs into life, I know what it's like to be one with a song, one with the One who has given the song, one with the ones who join in the song to ensure it will live on. This is synchronicity.

Synchronous connections permeate my life. Yesterday, for example, I picked up the phone. I just had to talk to a friend I hadn't heard from in a while. Before I could dial her number, it rang, and there she was. "I'm in the middle of a forest," she said. "How lovely!" I replied. "That's why I called," she said, amazed. "It's about your song, 'How Lovely.' What CD is it on?" Harmonic convergence. When was the last time it happened to you? If we pay attention we will discover it is happening all the time.

If synchronous links are indigenous to life, why are we constantly out of synch, not only with what is around us, but with an integral part of ourselves? Deep within all creation is a yearning to be connected, yet symptoms of disconnection are prevalent everywhere. We live in a frantic and fragmented world that has us running in all directions as we multitask and multiply responsibilities.

Sometimes we simply outrun ourselves, unable to keep up with producing or performing twenty-four/seven.

There are so many ways we cut ourselves off from sources of integration. We become estranged from someone we love, from our extended family, from team members or a group of peers, from those with whom we disagree, from one or more of the contexts in which we find ourselves each day. One way in which we disengage is to be over against someone we dislike or something counterproductive. Another is to demonize those whom we are inclined to reject. To overpower, take over, dominate, and destroy are characteristic of one who is set apart and resistant to being identified as part of a harmonious whole. We remain out of synch as long as we ignore that inner voice urging us to reconnect again.

Ironically the very structures that exist to draw us all together have also been instrumental in pulling us apart. Democracy, a unifying force for freedom and opportunity, seems far less concerned today about concealing its imperfections. To many of us it seems that it is becoming impervious to them. Our politics and our economy can be devious and divisive. We constantly shuffle priorities and we take for granted the coexistence of excessive wealth and a very vast and vulnerable underclass.

Religion also contributes to division and separation. So much of my religious formation consisted of being not for but against. To be a Christian meant being separated from all those who were not, and to be a Catholic meant being different from other Christians. We were conditioned to be in the world but not of the world. As a result, and in a variety of ways, we created a completely separate world as we awaited a world beyond this world and attempted to live as though we were already there in body and in spirit.

Fortunately, much of this has changed. What lingers, however, is an ambivalent relationship to the world that we have been called to transform. Despite all the good Christianity has been able to accomplish, a predominant feature continues to be its dominating, separatist side, which is often out of synch in a pluralistic context.

When it comes to the world around us, we need to reflect on boundaries, not the physical demarcations that overpower and subdivide, but those thin places etched in spirit on the tablets of the heart. Mine are permeable. I was always too connected to the soul of this world to ever be against it or to walk away from it, too caught up in its wonders, too utterly aware of a sacred Presence radiating everywhere. A very long time ago I was drawn deep into the heart of our world by our Creator's compassion for all that is and was and will be. "God so loved the world" has always been one of my favorite phrases.

The Spirit of God in the person of Jesus lived here with us as one of us and will remain among us always. Jesus, thoroughly immersed in this world, was concerned for all God's people, for the lilies of the field and the birds of the air, a testament to his love for all that exists this side of heaven.

It's a wonderful world indeed. Instead of letting go of that which I loved with a passion when I accepted my vocation, I embraced it more fully and far more intimately in the way contemplatives do. To be a child of God, a prophet of God, to be in love with God is to love all that God has created. We are made to be of one accord with all that has life and breath and being through a bond that transcends separation and is synchronous with grace.

The world is not a construct. It is a dynamic entity of cosmic energy. Planet Earth — Gaia — is a living organism made up of living organisms that are interacting and intersecting, evolving and adapting, self-sustaining yet interdependent, moving in and out of mutually beneficial relationships.

The whole is a whole lot more than the sum of its multiple parts. It is a model of synchronicity. We of the human species are a vital and very influential aspect of it all. When we strive to be cooperative, to be of one heart, one accord, one spirit, even as we continue to be different and disagree, we stabilize the planet in life-giving ways. Our harmonic vibrations are in synchronous phase and a pulsating lifeline channels healing and peace.

Synchronicity is a gift that arises from the spirit of a quantum universe. It is the Holy Spirit's way of integrating all.

Change

Those of us who have been formed within the constraints of a past paradigm continue to conform to its expectations and dance to the beat of its drum.

According to that mechanistic worldview, which is still prevalent, the bottom line for a stable society, or for any functional system, is for things to stay as they are. We have always done it this way, we have heard over and over again, which is to say that this is how it is going to remain. Regimentation and rigidity are the downside of this worldview. Order and productivity are the seductive outcomes sustaining it long after its time has passed.

In religion and society, change too often has threatened those who are in authority or have a vested interest in something under siege. To introduce deviation meant one might be labeled for life. Only renegades raised questions, only troublemakers stirred things up, only heretics, the devil's advocates, tampered with tradition and criticized the status quo. Equilibrium was the ideal, dependability the norm. To be placid on the surface sent a signal to those outside the system that things within were under control and that all was right with the world.

We who have worked so hard at becoming effective agents of change in a world that seemed distressingly stagnant were unprepared for the extent to which revolutionary change would occur. We did not anticipate the rapidity of the transition from pay phones and postage stamps to cellular and Web-based networking, and its global extent. Who could have known that this quantum leap in communications would be instantaneously ubiquitous and that those who would lead us into the future would create a new and interactive society coexistent with the old? In an electronic context, continuity and stability are difficult to imagine, and the call to conformity seems utterly absurd.

Spawned in a technological milieu, the grandchildren of the computer age are hardwired for change. This Internet-savvy population is adept at dealing with a swiftly moving pace and is constantly shifting gears. We who pleaded for innovation and launched movements that lobbied for change now struggle to avoid being overwhelmed by the awakening we had so ardently hoped for and ultimately affirm. We still have a lot to convey to present and future generations, but now it is less about shedding accretions and more about honoring eternal values that withstand the passage of time. First, however, we will have to learn to reinterpret and subsequently recast the essentials of faith and freedom in contemporary terms. As Teilhard de Chardin once said, prophetically: "Let us learn to orient our being in the flux of things."[40]

In a world that is rapidly changing and will always be in flux, rigidity is inappropriate and ultimately ineffective. It is not in our best interests to resist incremental changes or to quell rebellious behaviors or to steadfastly ignore the reasons why these things occur. A propensity to break the rules or to replace them with recommendations may not necessarily be negative actions. Rocking the boat, rattling the cage, upsetting the apple cart, blowing the whistle — once considered unacceptable behaviors — are looked upon now by many as inherent to our evolving.

Many of the systems that support us, as well as the philosophical rationale underlying our relationships in a globally oriented society, are out of synch with the dynamic and very real aspects of our day-to-day life. We need to revamp our infrastructures, physical and social, which have already begun to decay. Deep-seated discriminations and stark systemic exclusions based on a hierarchy of power are now in serious conflict with egalitarian movements and emerging aspirations, not only from within, but from far off corners of the world unaccustomed to conforming to a Western worldview.

We are on the cusp of a paradigm shift of gigantic proportions. In order to meet this challenge, some fundamental aspects of our way of life simply have to change. Unfortunately those structures that must evolve are under the control of forces that are most resistant to change. Consequently explosive counter-forces determined to precipitate this paradigm shift will continue to contribute to massive disfunction and debilitating disparity on a global scale while in pursuit of their goal.

We will not resolve this predicament by amassing more firepower or by gobbling up Earth's resources or by accumulating inordinate wealth or by perpetuating an unjust and inequitable distribution of life's necessities. In a world where there really is enough, any effort at globalization must ensure that there is enough for all.

Of this we can be certain. No one nation will get very far by going it alone. We are cognizant of all Earth's people now through our multifaceted connections and consequently aware of one another's needs. Therefore, the new paradigm will reflect the growing realization that we are all in this together. A shift in practice has to begin with a radical change in perception. The worldview that is emerging must be based on bedrock values and a cosmic orientation. A commitment to the survival and well-being of all life on and beyond our planet and our universe can be sustained only by a concomitant spirituality rooted in the conviction that we are all one in spirit because we are all reflections of that Being we call divine.

Daily we are emerging from an illusion of equilibrium into the whirligig phenomenon of change. It has been a rude awakening. There is nothing that we can point to and say, "This is impervious to change." Reality is not static. It is not an expanse of serenity interrupted by disarray, nor is it perpetual mayhem, but rather a dynamic engagement with life forces in and around us during which we are re-vitalized by interludes of stillness and steadfast stability that reverberate within.

We are only beginning to understand that from the moment of our conception we are constantly changing, and everything around us is changing along with us. Eventually we will realize that we have been given the wherewithal to thrive in this milieu, for we were not designed to be stoic but to be flexible while in flux.

While most traditions and many trends tend to counter-act quantum reality, reinforcing resistance to change, the universe continues to push us forward into a more dynamic and more comprehensive approach to life. In the process we are discovering there is much more to reality than what we were led to believe or will ever understand. That may be one of the reasons for the success of a virtual reality, one we have fooled ourselves into believing we can manipulate and control. It allows us to venture beyond the limits of what is acceptable, to rearrange the world for a little while before returning to the way it was before we ran away from it, and to the way we were. If reality shows and video games are any indication, we have some serious work to do if we are going to face reality and accept it for what it is.

The more we allow ourselves to become absorbed in un-reality, the harder it will be to face and consequently deal with those outcomes that await us in a world that is ex-cruciatingly real. There, when a full-blown crisis occurs, we think that, suddenly, everything has changed. Actu-ally, everything around us and everything within us has been changing all along. What is slow to change is the fact that we remain unaware of this. The findings of quantum physics suggest that past and future merge to create a perpetually changing now. Perhaps this is what we fear the most, this immersion in instability, where the tendency to be somewhat in control disappears in a vortex of change. Perhaps this is why so many good and godly people continue to cling so tenaciously to their old religious and patriotic ways and why so many young and vivacious leaders of the future are creating their own reality in preference to what they see.

What is alive is always changing. God is always changing. The universe and all its stars, exploding and expanding, are forever changing, and so are you and I. We cannot cling to that which is essentially ephemeral, except in the realm of energy and of spirit that abides. Let go of all that stands in the way of the impulse of creation and its existential flow. Change is the universal constant for everyone everywhere. In this lies our hope for a better future, and for a more just, more peaceful, and far more compassionate world.

Change is not only probable, it is absolutely certain, but the kind of change we are hoping for has to begin with us. In the words of Mohandas Gandhi: "You must be the change you wish to see in the world."[41] He was, and we can be too.

This is the Spirit's gift to us in an era of quantum awakening: the ability to live in the ebb and flow as centered, sentient beings, and the capacity to be and to become an example of and a catalyst for the transformation for which we long.

Chapter 9

Fruits of a Quantum Spirit

Civilization has always been preoccupied with results. The current term is "outcomes," but it is still the same. Be fruitful. Be successful. Be prolific. Produce. Cultivate the benefits. Show us what you can do. We have been evaluated, and subsequently validated, according to our productivity. We reap the rewards of the seeds we sow and we hope for a bountiful harvest. Some have more, some have less, and a lot will never have enough; but that is the overall result of the more recent mechanical model, which will eventually disappear in the wake of evolutionary change.

Quantum principles hint at a new worldview in the making, where spirituality that moves from the outside in will no longer make sense in the midst of all those transformative influences flowing from the inside out. We will be valued primarily for the quality of our participation within a diversified universe and for how we relate to other entities populating our cosmos. A quantum spirit is evocative of qualitative responses that enrich and energize. Where the fruitfulness of one becomes the mother lode of the many, the whole will be so much greater than all of its participating parts.

Fruits of the Spirit essential to an emerging spirituality in a quantum universe will be those dynamic qualities that compel us to probe our lived reality and be open to what we find. Four fruits featured in the reflections that follow remind us of what is precious to us. The four fruits are Continuity, Relationship, Wholeness, and Transformation. They are fundamental to what we cannot live without. In a world perpetually in flux, where change itself is constant, we need to focus now and then on tendencies that abide.

We also need to find ways to strengthen those tendencies in us. The following points for reflection may help and may even evoke a commitment to dig deeper into the four aspects of God's quantum Spirit offered for reflection here.

- Describe the thread of continuity weaving your life together. How will it change as you develop your spirituality in a quantum universe?

- Reflect on your capacity to enter into relationship with family, friends, and acquaintances, with the destitute and the stranger, with nature, and with God.

- Why does it make sense to say that we are all one? What does your life story contribute to the universe story? How can we be a vital part of one unified whole?

- What were some of the transformative turning points on your journey? What are some of the ways in which you hope to be transformed? Since transformation comes from within, how might you help it happen?

Continuity

I'm caught up in the latest episode of my favorite television show when suddenly, in the midst of a tantalizing scene, the screen goes blank. It says: "To be continued." I feel like someone has just stuck a pin in my balloon.

We don't like to be left hanging. We are frustrated when things remain unresolved because we anticipate continuity and some kind of conclusion. By setting goals and fulfilling an endless stream of expectations through the greater part of our lives, we have been programmed to finish what we start so we can start and finish something else in an uninterrupted cycle characteristic of the mechanical age and foundational to its achievements.

An orientation to continuity goes all the way back to prehistoric times. Prior to recorded history with its sense of forward progression, continuity was perceived as cyclical. The ancients found security in the cosmic blueprint left behind by the gods who had once inhabited Earth before moving on: the perennial return of the seasons; the rising and setting of the sun; the phases of the lunar cycle; the ebb and flow of oceanic tides; the repetitive rhythms of wind and rain; seed sown that comes to fruition; a yesterday to remember tomorrow; a newborn child to complete the cycle of birth, death, rebirth.

In one sense an expectation of a cosmic continuity can be a saving grace. It lets us pick up where we left off, creating the illusion that time and space are definitive of our universe, confirming traditional religious and cultural understandings of the whole. Biblical tradition is predicated on looking back and looking forward. We remember what God has done for us and order our present reality in anticipation of an endtime of unending bliss. This is still the predominant ethos, even though an emerging understanding of our quantum universe is challenging the conceptual framework taken for granted for so long.

Quantum physics has established that matter does not flow continuously and predictably according to the laws of motion that defined the mechanical era. It jumps from one place to another in a discontinuous manner. We live in a chaotic world of inexplicable discontinuity consisting of energy particles and waves that are constantly in motion and move in a random and seemingly disjointed series of leaps and bounds. How can this be, we ask, because this is not how we perceive it? There is a real world out there, we insist, one that is proof of some kind of physical and consistent continuity throughout the ages. When we consider life here on Earth from the perspective of what we have experienced during our limited lifespan, we conclude that continuity is at the core of what it means to be alive.

Nevertheless, this much is certain. Discontinuity has been proven to be fundamental to quantum physics and is therefore a fact of life. In the invisible subatomic realm at the heart of all that is, leaping matter and erratic motion are random and discontinuous. On the surface, however, our physical world appears continuous, and this is an equally valid view of the world in which we live. Reality consists of both the visible and the invisible, not only in our physical world, but our spiritual world as well. Quantum spirituality, like quantum reality, consists of what is seen and also that which is not seen, of continuity and discontinuity. Both play a role in the evolution and interpretation of life on our planet. Both continuity and discontinuity are actively shaping who we are.

One hardly needs to make a case for continuity. It is evident everywhere. Day after day, year after year, the tapestry of our lives is woven from what we have experienced, and we carry our past within us for as long as our spirit lives. We remain solidly entrenched in a presumption of continuity, which is why discontinuity often takes us by surprise. What doesn't fit the pattern to which we have become accustomed or departs from the way we think things should be is considered an aberration to be eliminated or overcome.

Discontinuity is disruption. However, it is also normative, only not to us, because we have not made room for it in our pantheon of possibilities. So what do we do about that? If discontinuity is a vital part of our natural world, and it is, and if it is endemic, then we need to begin to look for it and see it for what it is meant to be: a ripple of divine energy creating and re-creating every aspect of the universe, redesigning our journey, recreating us.

The more I think about it, the more I realize the overarching themes in the story of my life have been the result of quantum leaps that disrupted continuity and challenged me, time after time, to start all over again. Dislocation was not only physical. It was often theological, and more often philosophical, but always, once befriended, left me feeling like I had come home. For me, continuity is in the persistent pull of the Spirit, which may mean stepping onto a path and then ending up on another. Even this book is making its own way to the finish line, leaping beyond the cautious outline that tried in vain to contain it, because life in the Spirit happens as you are making other plans.

How are we to reconcile the principle of discontinuity with the unwavering certitude of our theological constructs? That is the question with which our quantum theologians will have to wrestle. The doctrinal frame congruent with a mechanical age of certainty in which there are things that never change poses limits that do not exist in a quantum universe. Many quantum scientists have been and continue to be women and men of faith whose relationship with the Divine has deepened as they struggled with these issues. At the core of quantum spirituality is one's consent to live the questions and to leave the answers to God.

Yes, the divine designer is disturbing and disruptive, expressive and explosive, a force for discontinuity, but also a wave of continuity weaving together all that was and already is and eventually will be. The Divine is the sacred spark that ignites and energizes creation, the fire within whereby we are able to let our own light shine. This is the treasure hidden in the field of energy coursing though us, the priceless pearl we keep searching for in the recesses of our heart. A remnant of the divine paradox is buried deep within us. Like leaven in a lifeless lump, this living witness to a sacred sanctuary animating vessels of clay is an eternity of continuity forever changing form.

Each of us is a syllable in the story we continue to tell. We are keepers of the memory, we who have heard the Spirit speak in whispers about these things. The memory of in the beginning has been handed down through the ages to those who have ears to hear the truth and the courage to proclaim it. Remember the mystery of God-with-us, the astonishing miracle of God-in-us. Remember, and pass it on.

Divine indwelling is our primary source of continuity, of Spirit speaking to spirit. As we heard Teilhard de Chardin say earlier, material energy and spiritual energy form a continuity and are active in the world.

This understanding of continuity is fruit of a quantum Spirit, and it is there for the taking during this transition time.

Relationship

We used to think that relationship was something exclusively human. By divine right it belonged to us. It gave us an edge in the rankings. The last shall be first, shall rise to the top, superior to all other forms of life.

Humanity lived accordingly. We exercised dominion and even claimed to have a preferential relationship with God. We thought that was how it had to be to fulfill our destiny. A growing number of us today don't think that way anymore. We have begun to re-vision our place within the universe story. As we move forward, the focal point will have to be relationship, where a paradigm shift in perception is already underway.

Quantum physics shattered an assumption foundational to our way of thinking, one that supports the frameworks of our theological and spiritual lives. Scientific findings verify that humans are not the only entities entering into relationship. The universe holds the copyright here, for long before our species evolved, that vast expanse of energy and matter was dynamically and chaotically in relationship within itself, and, as a person of faith I would add, with the Source that preconceived it.

From the beginning and for as long as whatever that exists continues to be, particles and waves of energy dance in and out of relationship, creating and recreating, effecting a fleeting yet lasting connection before moving on. Cosmology reveals we still have much to learn about relationship. The universe and its proxy, planet Earth, are waiting to share their wisdom and their experience with us.

For instance when particles of energy interact a connection is established that transcends astronomical distances.

This connection can be reactivated after the energy moves on, no matter how far into the future or how far away in space. Quantum energy is constantly moving in and out of relationship throughout the universe. It carries with it, like pollinating bees, like the consciousness of memory, those traces of what went before, a perennial potential for connectivity crisscrossing everywhere.

Particles and waves, constantly in motion, are moving in and out of us and in and out of everything and everyone everywhere. Each of us is bombarded by trillions of solar neutrinos daily, by elements of trees and hummingbirds and whatever aspects of God's creation make their way to where we are and into and out of our energy fields, leaving something behind. In some sense we harbor the sun and the moon and the stars in the cells within us, and on the cellular level, we are host to oceans and deserts and plains, to Africa and the Amazon, to Asia and the Arctic, to every place we have ever been and to everyone who has ever so briefly come across our path.

This cosmic web of relationships blows our previous understanding right off our mental map. It will take some major adjusting to come around to this way of relating. In fact, to arrive at such a radically reoriented perspective will require a quantum leap.

What might our world be like if every day we consciously acknowledged our relationship with creation and its relationship to us? Like those Native Americans who consider all creation to be "our relatives," let's solidify our relationships on nature's side of the family. Many of us have already found close friends and soul mates there.

Talk to the wind and listen as it whispers its secrets to you. Sing with the birds the songs that originated once upon a simpler time and let them take your soul's improvisations under their wing. Yes, hug a tree. Feel how it feels. Let mutual energies meet and merge as you lean into its branches and are tickled by its leaves. Wiggle your toes in the dew-laden grass and imagine a magic carpet transporting your spirit into the wild. Take time, when you wish upon a star, to tell the star what you wish for, and even seek to discern the source of the twinkle in its eye.

A part of us still runs with the wolves, still takes to the sea like a mermaid, and whenever we stand on the top of a hill just as the sun is setting, we know that we are cradled in those Everlasting Arms. Although we have evolved beyond the way we were in the dreamtime, we never outgrow our longing to take our place at the family gathering among our next of kin.

The gift the universe gives is a perspective on relationship. It sings to us of kinship with a life-giving energy extending the length and breadth of space that has no limitations and is welcoming of all. The universe is trying to tell us that we need to replicate this spirit in relationships of our own. What would it be like if we approached every new acquaintance as if we had met before? As if we had something in common. As if we were related. As if we were already friends. Can you imagine what this would do for planetary peace? There would be no point in building walls along our nation's borders when the walls within us that keep people out are finally coming down.

What can we give back to the universe that has given so much to us? We offer a sense of relationship that is shaped by our humanity, an awareness of the necessity for relationships with depth. Our gift is a hunger for connections that are loving and lasting. For us a genuine relationship is more than a passing encounter or a momentary hookup before moving on. We have our own share of one-night stands, but these are seldom satisfying. The desire to remain connected and the joy that comes with intimacy fulfill that dimension of the Divine we share with a loving God. Our gift is also a consciousness of being in relationship, the knowledge of what is unfolding, of what has been and what might be. This awareness carries the responsibility of using our God-given gifts to foster interconnectivity in ways that will contribute to planetary justice and peace.

An understanding of relationship from a quantum perspective is crucial to the evolution of our present age. The universe tells us to broaden our scope. Humanity says, go deeper. Form relationships with depth. To develop both in a way that precipitates the good that we envision can only come from a broader and deeper relationship with the Divine. The universe reflects an archive of images of that divine reality some of us call God. Incarnate divinity inhabits nature in a kaleidoscope of forms. When we are close to nature, we are close to God.

O Thou who created the universe and all that we see on our planet, we worship your pulsating presence in all that you have made. You are the sun and the moon and the stars. You are the wind and the water. You are in all that you have made and all you have made is in you. We thank you for the myriad ways we see you, name you, know you, even though our human consciousness cannot grasp your cosmic Presence, for you are so much greater than our capacity to be aware. Surely our fixation on controlling the ways we relate to you is like canonizing a single grain in a Sahara of sand. Only our need to return to our source makes any sense of our efforts. Only your infinite patience gives us the courage to reach out to you over and over again.

A world of peace and prosperity for all inhabitants of planet Earth can and will come to fruition through rock-solid relationships. Cross-cultural and interfaith relationships, personal and social relationships are ways whereby we replicate our relationship with the Divine.

Relationship is a succulent and savory fruit of our quantum Spirit. The proof is in the experience. Spirit invites us to taste and see.

Wholeness

It is all of a piece, our universe, together with whatever else exists in that unexplored expanse of space beyond our technological probes with their telescopic eyes. Eruptions and spiral orbits, expansion and contraction, galaxies and supernovas, planets, comets, and asteroid belts and new moons and aging stars are all an integral part of a living and moving work of art.

It is a stellar performance, a billion times more wondrous than anything we might imagine. Light and darkness, fire and ice, chaos and serenity, intersecting fields of energy, life, death, new life, more death, creation and destruction, history and mystery, creativity and serendipity flowing forth from the love of God. All is interconnected in this cosmic tapestry.

But wait — a quixotic anomaly is spinning around in this vast milieu. A solitary renegade, and there may be many more. In the crook of our Milky Way's spiral arm, a rogue planet, warmed by its sun, rotates on its axis, considering its place in the scheme of things, relishing it all.

It is all of a piece, our planet. A galactic canopy encircles Earth, and clouds, gravitational forces, and electromagnetic energy. Fire and oil and water and rock and precious gems and so much more lie hidden deep within. On the surface, all forms of life, teeming, scheming, dreaming as natural and human resources seek to sustain the universe's evolutionary experiment.

All is interconnected. All of this is one. Gaia, a living entity, breathes and weeps and procreates, presenting to the universe a geological and biological organism with a genealogy of its own. How blessed are we to be a part, albeit an infinitesimal part of Earth's identity. When we immerse ourselves in the swirling waters of our beloved planet — its seas, rivers, lakes, streams, and tumbling waterfalls — when we splash in its puddles after the rain, how often do we remember that these are the natal waters that opened the gates of our mother's womb to trumpet our arrival, that continue to ebb and flow within us, diluting our tears, slaking our thirst, cleansing us and refreshing us inside and out? Flames that reduce our forests to ash are the fire in the belly of our becoming. Wind that shakes the acorns free, rocks the cradle, fells the pine as it blows, blusters, whispers, wails, is breath of life, breath of the Spirit, life force linking all that inhales and exhales existence. So much more than stardust seals our genetic link to the universe. We are immersed in the energies that circulate from the frontiers of space, integrating all.

It is all of a piece, the genetic map that traces genus and species. We humans are kin to all on our planet and cousin to every magnificent creature that evolved in its own way. The roundworm left its mark within us, and when we look in the mirror we see a primate looking back.

We are siblings of one another, we of the human species, for we are one family of brothers and sisters populating planet Earth, sharing a genetic history, evolving from a common source before taking divergent paths. When we look into a stranger's eyes, we see they are similar to our own, and if we linger we may even see the residual light of a star.

> The world filled by God appears to our enlightened eyes as simply a setting in which universal communion can be attained.[42]

That is how Teilhard de Chardin describes it, but this sense of cosmic oneness is not limited to mystics. We can feel the heartbeat of life itself pulsate throughout the planet whenever we take another's hand and acknowledge that we are one. How, then, can we fail to recognize that our multifaceted diversity is a prism of the Divine?

> With terror and intoxicating emotion, I realized that my own poor trifling existence was one with the immensity of all that is and all that is still in process of becoming.[43]

It is all of a piece, for all is connected within the divine milieu. We are immersed in the sacred. Everywhere we choose to go, we walk on holy ground. The soul of the universe is divinity present everywhere and in everything, in you and me, in friend and foe, and in all who share our sacred space on our hallowed planet. We are vessels of a holy spirit, channels of a sanctifying grace, called to proclaim a liberating word, to be a healing presence, to love as we are loved by everlasting Love.

The intriguing part of freedom is that we can choose to be part of the whole in ways that support and sustain it, or we can opt to cut ourselves off from the ebb and flow of goodness through choices that destroy. This either/or is really both/and, for that which heals and that which harms are integrated, matter and form, into one undivided whole. Those who are against me are part of me and that which needs redemption is but a cosmic moment away from succumbing to transforming forces that swirl around and within a sacrosanct milieu.

Subatomic particles moving in and out of relationship carry good memories far and wide as sacramental blessing. Energy traverses the universe to pass through me and into you, so a part of me is a part of you and a bit of us both moves on and into someone somewhere else, perhaps even half a world away. My enemy and I are one. The bombs that destroy a villager's home will explode inside my heart.

Because it is all of a piece, we need to change our piece-meal approach to addressing global issues and planetary concerns. We cannot carry on in isolation nor fix only one piece of the puzzle and forget about the rest. We need to re-image and re-imagine how we are going to proceed in a world that is constantly evolving. As we continue to speak metaphorically of building a better world, we need to reflect on how this metaphor fits within a quantum perspective, where building implies putting together some-thing from separate parts. Constructing anything piece by piece is iconic of a past paradigm, like taking a text out of context and failing to recognize its place within the larger story and the overarching story's relationship to our own.

When we seek to repair or heal or adjust or influence a particular part of the whole, we must always remain aware of the whole and its relationship to its parts, for the whole preexists the sum of its parts within a quantum framework. We can and do affect the whole by interacting with one of its elements, as quantum theory contends. It may seem on the surface that nothing has occurred, but once energy is set in motion, a process for systemic change has begun, for the tiniest local interaction can have a very broad effect.

What is a fact for science is an element of faith for spirituality. There has been a distinct separation between science and spirituality, but not anymore. Scientific perceptions and the worldviews of the ancients, of the mystics and the sages, are beginning to converge. There are quantum physicists who say that reality is undivided.

The inseparable quantum interconnectedness of the whole universe is the fundamental reality.[44]

Physicist David Bohm insists that, despite its segmentation, our world is a seamless whole, that an inherent unity underlies all our diversity and the illusion of our separateness. "Wholeness is what is real," he says. Our "habitual fragmentation" and its tendency "to divide everything from everything" must come to an end.[45] Indeed, "science itself is demanding a new, non-fragmentary world view."[46]

The classical idea of the separability of the world into distinct but interacting parts is no longer valid or relevant. Rather, we have to regard the universe as an undivided and unbroken whole.[47]

Chinese philosopher Lao Tzu taught:

> The Nameless is the origin of Heaven and Earth;
> The Name is the mother of all things.
> The two are the same, but after they are produced,
> they have different names.[48]

The *Tao*, a kind of cosmic flow, is the universal reality unifying all. This reiterates the ancient Greek perception of reality as unbroken wholeness. It is also the vision of Jesus, this sense that all is connected, that all that exists is one:

> That they may be one, as we are one . . . that they may all be one; as you are in me and I am in you, may they also be in us. . . . that they may be one, as we are one, I in them and you in me, that they may become completely one.[49]

These sentiments of Jesus were not limited to his immediate disciples. Jesus envisions a wider circle and evokes the dawn of a new creation where all are a part of the divine Creator's all-encompassing milieu. The universe confirms this. Therefore all our efforts to separate, segregate, and set apart will be to no avail. At the heart of a spirituality shaped by a quantum universe is the conviction that all are one.

Today planet Earth, like Noah's ark, is adrift in turbulent waters. The rising tides of economic and environmental discontent threaten to overwhelm our frantic efforts to stay afloat. It is time to stop making enemies and start making friends. We have to remind ourselves that we are all in this boat together, and it will take all our ingenuity to make it to higher ground. There the lion's share of the blessings will equal that of the lamb's, and the well-being of our planet will be the concern of all.

Our multicolored rainbow is a reminder that once the floodwaters had abated in the Genesis story, God made a covenant with all creation, with the seas, the trees, the stones, the stars, and with every living creature, and with every one of their descendants in future generations. Today the rainbow is the sign of that everlasting covenant between God and planet Earth, with all who call this planet home and the whole of its cosmic context. It tells us to remember that within the community of all beings a loving energy permeates all and sustains the divine milieu.

We are forever inundated with that which is wholly other and yet tantalizingly near. This, the matrix of our wholeness, is why all are one.

Transformation

For a while, in certain circles, a lot was said about transformation. The word appeared in vision statements. For some it became a goal. It seemed every time we turned around something, or someone, had recently been transformed. That would have been good news, really, if only it were so, but transformation does not happen when and where we want it to or because we aim to bring it about by the end of a calendar year.

A lot of good and significant change has occurred in recent decades, yet we know from our deepest needs and dreams that little has been transformed. As with hope and our loftier aspirations, here our reach exceeds our grasp, but we keep on reaching anyway. We do so because we must. A force within the universe and deeply encoded in all of us compels us to keep pushing forward into ever new realizations. Transformation marks milestones on the path of evolution. It is nature's persistent, triumphant aha! It is God's perennial surprise.

There is another word for this. "Metamorphosis." It means a substantive change in structural form and function. This is happening all around us in our physical world. The tadpole becomes a frog, the caterpillar a butterfly with brightly colored wings. Science is finding more evidence to support the outrageous assertion that birds evolved from dinosaurs. What a transformation! The same can be said about us from a biological perspective, for we have apes and gorillas and chimps clinging to our family tree.

Metanoia is yet another way of saying transformation. I heard this a lot as a novice in formation for a vowed life as a missionary who was somewhat monastic. Metaphysically, it is a conversion experience whereby the mind and one's way of life are radically and substantially changed. This type of change goes way beyond changes, which is something I had to learn. More than once I thought I was on the verge of stepping over the threshold into transformation. When I put on the habit and veil and, again, when I made perpetual vows, I wasn't the person I had been before because far more than the framework had changed. However, I came to realize that a full-blown transformation does not occur with a change of clothing or a life-changing commitment, no matter how profound.

When a feminist perspective clicked deep within, re-orienting everything, when I started to see the world differently and myself in a whole new way, when faith lines and bloodlines blurred and bonds of relationship intensified in the wake of a quantum awakening, I could feel transforming energy pulling me closer to the brink. Yet always, I could look back and realize that I was not yet there.

I have grown beyond the boundaries defining me spiritually and theologically. I have changed significantly after shedding all kinds of protective cocoons; but no matter how high my spirit soars, I remain this side of the veil. My total transformation is not for here but for the hereafter. Some may prefer a halo. I'm waiting for my wings.

Focusing on the systemic, what can we say about changes that have occurred in the world around us during our own lifetime? Which of the seismic shifts that mark historic, decisive turning points reflect transformation? We have yet to put an end to war after centuries of armed combat. The number of impoverished people, particularly children, who are hungry and often homeless, locally and on a global scale, continues to rise. The *aggiornamento* of Vatican II did not leave the Catholic Church transformed despite all those radical changes. This is clear from its moral rejection of lesbians and gays and from its refusal to ordain women and to accept married priests, even as parishes close and communities are deprived of Eucharist.

So what are we to do? Does this mean that all our efforts to bring about a transformation of religion and society are frivolous and futile? Does it mean that our dreams of living in a more peaceful and compassionate world will forever be like dust and ashes blowing in the wind? No, not exactly.

Let transformation be the light that leads our ship to harbor. Let it be that sense of urgency that will not let us rest in peace until global peace prevails. As we go about our works of mercy, remember, we are conduits for a divine energy; we are catalysts of a holy spirit. Transformation can be triggered, but we cannot know for certain when it will arrive. That would be like setting a deadline for finding the Holy Grail. Nor can results be measured. That would be like holding the light from a star in the palm of our hand.

Transformation is elusive. Even when it does kick in, not many will perceive it, but its blessings will affect the lives of future generations. This is where a quantum perspective can help us keep on giving our all without ever giving up, because in a quantum universe, that's the way it is.

One of the challenges we face in stirring up transformative energy is that few people know what we're talking about. Popular culture co-opted transformation and cut it off from its spiritual source, equating it with a total makeover of one kind or another. This understanding has been carried over from a past paradigm, where any change of significance is imposed from outside the system and is then carefully regulated according to established norms.

Having a makeover is light years removed from the ontological reality of a metaphysical transformation. The one is superficial. The other is profound. One is imposed strategically from without, while the other works organically from within, remaining inner-directed because it originates within.

Transformation begins with a small disturbance or deviation within the self or the system, which inevitably leads to change. Seemingly insignificant changes can have astonishing effects. Changes start to accumulate until, at some unpredictable point, an entity is transformed.

Bit by bit, on a cellular level, we are all being transformed, for transformation is an organic process inherent in everything. When I left home at a very young age, inexperienced and unknowing, I entered into a wider world that entered into me. I was never the same again. Every subsequent step of my journey, every radical shift in consciousness, every song I sang, every song I sing has sown a potentially transformative seed somewhere on our planet that one day will bear fruit. Each generous deed anyone does, every act of loving kindness, every selfless stand for justice goes spiraling out to affect or influence reality at its core.

Bit by bit the energy flows. Bit by bit the awareness grows. Transformational energy is chaotically accumulating and exponentially replicating. When it reaches the tipping point, something — someone — somewhere, will be transformed.

We are standing at a crossroad. The way it has been is behind us. What will be lies ahead. The stone that sealed the tomb of Jesus before it was rolled away has ricocheted onto our landscape and is blocking our capacity to embrace the fullness of life. We who are Easter people are deeply mired in a culture of death. Until we own up to our role in the decimation that abounds, neither we, nor those we fight or fear, will ever be transformed.

Many of our behaviors endanger the life of our planet and stifle the hopes of its people. As surely as dawn dispels the darkness, these too will one day be extinct. If dinosaurs can morph into birds and delight us with their music, then we can and will evolve in ways that equip us for that bold new world spinning all around us. We can start now to participate in our own transformation by turning our swords into plowshares and our bullying words into song.

Chapter 10

Paradoxology

I did not know what I was getting into when I hooked up with *para*. I did not realize it would lead to the brink of a quantum universe, where I would be given what I needed to take a quantum leap of faith into its expanse.

At first I thought it all began when *para* landed in my lap with paradoxology, but it was I who landed in the lap of *para* when I was still in pigtails and just beginning to learn the steps of its metaphysical dance. I was enamored with paradox long before I stumbled onto paradoxology and fell into the vortex where paradigm and paradox collaborate or collide. The word to define those early experiences would come decades later, but the influence of paradoxology on my spirit's journey began philosophically with pencil and paper in a minuscule garden nestled against a saloon.

My lifelong love affair with words, their syllable sounds, their rhythms and rhymes, their capacity to capture what I beheld, imaginatively or actually, so that what I experienced could be kept forever in my heart, began with a simple poem I wrote many years ago. My first grade teacher introduced me to the magic of metaphor. She showed me how something could also be, simultaneously, something else, and only the Spirit of God knows why that made good sense to me. A play on words let me play with words in ways that helped prepare me for a quantum universe, where what you see is not what you get, because so much of what you get you can never really see, and what you see may not necessarily be what it really is.

In my parallel universe I encountered paradox again and again, inviting it to come closer, until it was part of me. In that embrace I fell in love with the metaphysical mysteries that hovered just beyond my grasp and eluded my understanding. I heard the call of the Spirit, and knew that, forever after, I would be led down labyrinthian paths, and I would not go alone.

Deep within creation there abides a quantum Spirit emanating from the Divine. Spirit was there in the beginning of the evolution of the cosmos, breathing life into every facet of everything that came after, as ubiquitous as air. Spirit was there at the beginning of my spiritual transformation, blowing through me like wind through a flute, giving vibrancy to the ephemeral and vitality to the invisible, like wind beneath my wings. I have grown by leaps and bounds beyond a lot of my limitations, as bit by bit, a paradoxical Spirit gave me paradoxology and the book that would bear its name. True to quantum reality, what began with writing a manuscript ended up rewriting a life. The paradigm shift still taking place is affecting everything.

Quantum theory offers a lens for another look at the way things are. It gives support to the heart's desire to be all encompassing and provides some evocative metaphors for making all things new. Who is God for me, and others, and where does the sacred begin or end are questions we cannot answer, but nevertheless must ask. In a quantum universe, where the how and why are always in flux, we also have to be ready to change along with our changing times. Quantum spirituality contributes a flexible framework for dealing with such things.

Faith, hope, and love are sacraments in a quantum society. They provide us with the ways and means of celebrating the liturgy of life, not through rites of privilege but through rituals of promise that arise out of our ordinary everyday routine and the surprises inherent within it.

Faith grounds us firmly in the matrix of the divine milieu, so that we can continue steadfast when buffeted by self-doubt, or when we are accused of losing our faith just when we are finding ways of living our faith more fully.

Hope is what we hang on to when we get up in the morning. It is what we cannot afford to let go of when everything else is gone. It is what we turn to when all other means of survival have been exhausted, the stepping stone to deliverance that tomorrow will build upon.

Love is all that really matters. Love is patient. Love is kind. Love is pathway to compassion and how justice is defined.[50] Every act of kindness, every gesture of compassion, the tiniest touch of tenderness is fractal of the one Great Love from whom all love spills over and to whom all love returns.

The physical world is our primary source of Spirit and spirituality in our quantum universe, and our spirituality is manifested, visibly and concretely, through who we are and how we behave. There is no longer a definitive separation between physical and metaphysical, the embodied and the ephemeral, visible and invisible. In the quantum paradox, natural and supernatural, once thought to be mutually exclusive, trade places, bait and switch, meet and even merge.

Einstein never could condone quantum's random reality, but as long as he lived he continued to remain affiliated with quantum theory. According to one of his well-known opinions, "God does not play dice with the universe."[51] Well, maybe God does. Suppose there is more to the impetuousness of haphazard random movement and the disorderliness of chance then what we have concluded. If so, the mystical heart will discern it long before more rational minds update their data banks.

In a quantum universe, we encounter a new relationship between in and out, up and down, here and there, was and is. Opposites do not repel or simply exist as one or the other. Sometimes they intermingle or meld and then move apart. Often they are one and the same. We will soon be able to count the ways that quantum spirituality reflects these characteristics. The relationship between center and edge is already one of them.

Our national and religious ideologies, mired in past paradigms, still hold a central position. Most people prefer the center, until we finally get there and learn it isn't what we thought it would be. We may end up stuck in stasis, like a traffic jam on the fourth of July, with nothing moving forward, and a whole lot of hanging around, while a surge of quantum energy is stirring along the edge.

A pioneering spirit is considered cutting edge, where movements often originate, where energy accumulates, where taking risks is no big deal, where people connect with other people to accomplish what is worthwhile.

At the edge you can see the horizon. Because it keeps on moving, you are never standing still, never claustrophobic, and you never feel hemmed in. You are free to stick your neck out without a gazillion opinions predisposed to lop it off.

The potency of a quantum universe amasses along the edge. The birth of a star or a galaxy begins at the rim of a black hole where energy is chaotic. The eruption of every supernova is the center of the universe, for the cosmic center is at the edge of something coming forth. The full force of its energy gives new meaning to creative edge.

Likewise we are at the center when we are at our creative edge. Being "at the center" is not the same as being "in the center" or "self-centered." When we reach deep within in order to center on something beyond ourselves, we become one with that central force of everlasting love.

It is necessary to recenter where energy flows freely. It is time to reconsider recentering at the edge. In an age of paradox, it is perfectly acceptable to relocate the center and redefine the edge.

We have a responsibility to help take the edge off hunger and the crucifying poverty that affects whole populations. This calls for new and creative ways of being in relationship with those who need what we have to offer. It is up to every one of us to be on that cutting edge. This means putting other people's needs at the center of our concern. We will have to begin by turning traditional priorities upside down and procedures inside out. We will have to convince controlling forces that the way they said things had to be doesn't have to be that way at all.

Who we are and what we believe and what we hope to give back to our world that has given so abundantly to us are dynamic moves in a delicate dance between being and becoming. In the world that is emerging, each of us is a shining star spinning circles in the cosmos. The good we do as we go along will go spiraling on forever, joining a retinue of blessings that is eternally expanding. This is the essence of prayer and praise. This is paradoxology. Think about this, and dance.

I am captivated by an image flitting in and out of my energy field. Here is what I imagine: the Spirit of the living God — and me — break-dancing on the edge.

As many more join in the dance — young and old, rich and poor, from every culture and cult and class — the growing, free-flowing energy will eventually reach its tipping point, spilling over to renew us all.

It is in and through the Spirit that the experiences of a lifetime, especially those we cannot understand, transcend the limits of our theology to reveal what they really are: genuine theophany, encounters with the sacred, shards of amazing grace. Here is where we hear God's call to be agents of wholeness and healing in a war-weary, war-wary, war-wasted world. How will we know if the call is genuine? In a quantum context, nothing is ever certain, but a blessed sense of assurance often accompanies uncertainty, along with an element of anticipation inherent in being unsure.

Life is a jigsaw puzzle. Sometimes the piece that is missing is the reason we keep going on. A whole lot has to fall into place before we are able to more fully grasp the meaning of a quantum universe. We cannot wait for that to happen before we start to shape a spirituality congruent with our quantum times.

Quantum spirituality is intrinsically cosmic. It sinks its roots in the paradoxical gifts and fruits of a quantum Spirit and is identified with life that is lived with acute integrity.

Once and for all it will dispel dysfunctional misunderstandings that cling to matter and spirit, accomplishing what the Spirit incarnate in Jesus intended to do.

It will build upon the received tradition's ancient quantum elements, as preserved in the sacred stories of the pregnancy of a village girl, the mysterious birth of her baby, the miracles attributed to her Spirit-filled child, his resurrection appearances after he was dead and buried, his ascension to another plane, and the Pentecostal experiences of a chastened community mystified en masse by an overpowering grace. It will liberate the prophetic energy restrained by canonically sanctioned sources and their interpretations, releasing the potential of Pentecost pent up within.

Jesus called this paradoxical wave the reign of God among us. Quantum spirituality calls it paradoxology. The Spirit of God and the spirit of Jesus are one quantum Spirit, and that Spirit is in us, and within all creation. The paradox of Jesus pervades paradoxology and is a spirit-linking force for global unity.

As I listen to God's loving and liberating Spirit, an underlying wisdom seems to be saying this.

Everything is relative. All knowledge of God is relative. Only God is Absolute and knows God absolutely.

Everything is energy. Chunks of quantum energy. Waves and fields of energy. Divine, creative energy forever evoking energy through God-Spirit permeating all.

Everything is connected. All energy is connected, woven into a pulsating, ever-changing web of life.

Paradoxology orients us in a quantum universe, providing a roadmap through paradox by showing us there are other ways of seeing what we fail to see, of comprehending what we cannot understand.

Paradoxology invites us into a new way of being in the world and in the process instills in us a radically reoriented perception and a fully inclusive worldview. At its core is this incomprehensible fact: there is nowhere that God is not.

Paradoxology signifies awareness of a pervasive quantum Spirit, creating and sustaining, incarnate and made manifest, source of our doxology and steadfast faithfulness, revealing: all are one.

Paradoxology, paradoxically, is how we can "pray always," in and through the physical world out there all around us and the invisible world that is in us. All that exists, because it exists, vibrates with an uninterrupted, all-inclusive energy proclaiming unequivocally: everywhere the Presence, and the glory, and the praise.

"Glory be!" our spirits cry, grateful for our blessings. What a grace it is to realize we are saturated with divinity, that our universe is securely anchored in its ebb and flow, that we, mere mortals, mingle and merge with the rippling tides of immortality, this moment, and forever.

Notes

1. Lewis Carroll, *Alice's Adventures in Wonderland and Through the Looking Glass* (New York: Lancer Books, 1968). *Looking Glass,* chapter 5. *Alice's Adventures* was first published in 1865.

2. Deepak Chopra, *Quantum Healing: Exploring the Frontiers of Mind/Body Medicine* (New York: Bantam Books, 1989), 170.

3. J. C. Chatterji, *The Wisdom of the Vedas* (Wheaton, Ill.: Quest Books, 1992), 30–31. This classic text was first published in 1931.

4. I first came across this term in Nick Herbert, *Quantum Reality: Beyond the New Physics* (New York: Anchor Books, 1985), 40. He writes: "It's beginning to look as if everything is made of one substance — call it 'quantumstuff.'"

Other helpful resources: Fritjof Capra, *The Tao of Physics: An Exploration of the Parallels between Modern Physics and Eastern Mysticism* (Boston: Shambhala, 2000); Donna Eden with David Feinstein, *Energy Medicine* (New York: Putnam, 1998); Kenneth Ford, *The Quantum World: Quantum Physics for Everyone* (Cambridge, Mass.: Harvard University Press, 2004); Stephen W. Hawking, *The Theory of Everything: The Origin and Fate of the Universe* (Beverly Hills, Calif.: New Millennium Press, 2002); James Lovelock, *The Ages of Gaia: A Biography of Our Living Earth* (New York: Bantam, 1988); J. P. McEvoy and Oscar Zarate, *Introducing Quantum Theory* (New York: Totem Books, 1996); Diarmuid O'Murchu, *Quantum Theology: Spiritual Implications of the New Physics* (New York: Crossroad, 1997); Brian Swimme and Thomas Berry, *The Universe Story* (San Francisco: HarperSanFrancisco, 1992); Evan Harris Walker, *The Physics of Consciousness: Quantum Minds and the Meaning of Life* (New York: Basic Books, 2000); Margaret J. Wheatley, *Leadership and the New Science: Learning about Organization from an Orderly Universe* (San Francisco: Berrett-Koehler Publishers, 1992); Fred Alan Wolf, *Taking the Quantum Leap: The New Physics for Non-Scientists* (New York: Harper & Row, 1981); Danah Zohar, *The Quantum Self: Human Nature and*

Consciousness Defined by the New Physics (New York: Quill/William Morrow, 1990); Gary Zukav, *The Dancing Wu Li Masters: An Overview of the New Physics* (New York: Quill/William Morrow, 1979).

5. Nelle Morton, *The Journey Is Home* (Boston: Beacon Press, 1985), 202.

6. Albert Einstein to Heinrich Zangger on Quantum Theory, May 20, 1912.

7. Richard Feynman, as cited in Herbert, *Quantum Reality*, xiii.

8. Wolf, *Quantum Leap*, xiv.

9. Albert Einstein. To date, efforts to discover the source of this very popular quote have not been successful.

10. Traditional tune: "Row, Row, Row Your Boat." It can be sung in unison and in a two-, three-, or four-part round. Text: Miriam Therese Winter, copyright © Medical Mission Sisters 2007.

11. Pierre Teilhard de Chardin, *Hymn of the Universe* (New York: Harper & Row, 1961), 36.

12. *The Great Catechesis of Gregory of Nyssa,* chapter 25.

13. Hagar, Genesis 16:13; Shaddai, Genesis 49:25, the first of many references in Hebrew Scripture.

14. In Matthew Fox, *Meditations with Meister Eckhart: A Centering Book* (Santa Fe: Bear & Co., 1983), 22.

15. Hildegard of Bingen, *Liber divinorum operum* (Book of divine works), Patrologia Latina, vol. 197.

16. From the author's book, *WomanPrayer, WomanSong: Resources for Ritual* (Eugene, Ore.: Wipf & Stock, 2008), 64; first published in 1987 by Meyer-Stone, then by Crossroad.

17. Sallie McFague, *The Body of God: An Ecological Theology* (Minneapolis: Fortress Press, 1993), ix.

18. Pierre Teilhard de Chardin, *The Divine Milieu* (New York: Harper & Row, 1960), 92.

19. Ibid., 89.

20. "Web of Life," words and music by Miriam Therese Winter, copyright © Medical Mission Sisters 2006.

21. Joseph Campbell, *The Power of Myth*, with Bill Moyers (New York: Doubleday, 1988), 32.

22. Teilhard de Chardin, *Hymn of the Universe*, 87.

23. Among Polynesian and Melanesian peoples, *mana* is a supernatural power or force, either good or evil, said to dwell within a person or an object.

24. Masaru Emoto, *The Hidden Messages in Water*, trans. David A. Thayne (New York: Atria Books, 2005.)

25. Edward Lorenz, who is known as the father of chaos theory.

26. *Washington Post* (October 31, 2006).

27. Lyall Watson, "The Biology of Being: A Natural History of Consciousness," in *The Spirit of Science*, ed. David Lorimer (New York: Continuum, 1999), 167.

28. Teilhard de Chardin, *Hymn of the Universe*, 94.

29. John Muir (1838–1914), conservationist and founder of the Sierra Club, considered a "wilderness prophet" and "citizen of the universe." *www.sierraclub.org.*

30. Title of a play by John Guare (1990), which was adapted to film (1993) and explores the premise that we are all connected to everyone else in the world by a chain of no more than six acquaintances; based on the "small world experiment" of Stanley Milgram, in which he examines the average path length for social networks in the United States.

31. In Daniel Ladinsky, *Love Poems from God: Twelve Sacred Voices from the East and West* (New York: Penguin 2002), 129.

32. "To Whom Shall We Go?" words and music by Miriam Therese Winter, copyright © Medical Mission Sisters 2006.

33. "Spirit of God," words and music by Miriam Therese Winter. copyright © Medical Mission Sisters 1965, 2002.

34. "Candles," text by Miriam Therese Winter, copyright © Medical Mission Sisters 2002.

35. Resetting of an earlier psalm by the author with similar cadence and several shared phrases.

36. "Light a Candle," words and music by Miriam Therese Winter, copyright © Medical Mission Sisters 2002.

37. An explanation of relativity that Einstein allegedly had his secretary give to nonscientists, as quoted in *Simpson's Contemporary Quotations*, compiled by James B. Simpson, 1988.

38. An assertion attributed to Anselm, popularized by Karl Barth.

39. See Larry Dossey, *Prayer Is Good Medicine* (San Francisco: HarperSanFrancisco, 1996).

40. Teilhard de Chardin, *Divine Milieu*, 84.

41. Efforts to find the source of this widely circulated quote by Gandhi have not been successful.

42. Teilhard de Chardin, *Science and Christ* (New York: Harper & Row, 1968), 168.

43. Teilhard de Chardin, *Writings in Time of War,* trans. Rene Hague (New York: Harper & Row, 1968), 25.

44. David Bohm, "On the Intuitive Understanding of Nonlocality as Implied by Quantum Theory," *Foundations of Physics* 5 (1975): 96, 102.

45. David Bohm, *Wholeness and the Implicate Order* (New York: Routledge, 1980), 7, 11.

46. Ibid., xi.

47. Ibid., 124–25.

48. Lao Tzu, a contemporary of Confucius in sixth-century B.C.E. China, wrote the *Lao Tzu,* also called *Tao-te ching* (Classic of the Way and its virtue), which played a distinctive role in the development of Taoist philosophy. Cited here are the opening lines (verse 1) as they appear in *The Great Asian Religions: An Anthology,* compiled by Wing-tsit Chan, Isma'il Ragi al Faruqi, Joseph M. Kitagawa, and P. T. Raju (New York: Macmillan Company 1969), 151.

49. John 17:21–23. Also see John 14:20.

50. From "Hymn to Love," by Miriam Therese Winter, copyright © Medical Mission Sisters 1995.

51. Common paraphrase for Albert Einstein's comment in a letter to Max Born (December 4, 1926) in *The Born–Einstein Letters,* trans. Irene Born (New York: Walker and Company, 1971).